ReMarkable

ReMarkable

THE GRIT AND GRACE
OF MARK CLIFTON

• • •

Dr. Judith K Werner

ISBN: 1544075464
ISBN 13: 9781544075464

Table of Contents

Acknowledgments

• • •

WITHOUT MARK AND NANCY CLIFTON, this book would never have existed; I wish with all my heart that what they and their two children endured had never occurred. But life doesn't work that way, and the pain they all went through became my story to tell. I am grateful to all four of them for the privilege of telling it.

It goes without saying that Mark's physicians were miracle workers and his multitudes of caregivers, friends, and other family members were support-givers without equal. As the book took shape, it was a pleasure to speak again to each doctor, technician, and therapist named herein. Each one agreed without question to my using his or her name and the part each played in Mark's battle. They all have the highest regard for their patient, Mark Clifton, and I am proud to be the one to tell his story. For the book, I used my own notes, hospital records, Nancy's CaringBridge posts, texts, emails, and discussions with his doctors and other family members to corroborate what I recalled. Any errors are mine alone.

I am also grateful for my two faithful former English majors who served me so well, evaluating the manuscript before it went off to the editor. One is my daughter, Carol Gustavson, now an attorney, and Cathy Kelly, now my CPA. Amazing what former English majors can do.

My most heartfelt thanks goes to my editor, Karen Rodgers, for her expertise, patience, and guidance, offered to another former English major, me. Without her, I'd still be back at the computer, wondering what to do next.

Introduction

• • •

FIRST I WAS AN ENGLISH teacher; then I became a physician. Later, I met Mark Clifton, who went from being a guy dating my daughter, to becoming one of my patients, to becoming one of my cancer patients, to becoming my son-in-law, to becoming the father of my two youngest grandchildren, to becoming all of the above, but fighting for his life. My unique vantagepoint allowed me early on to develop a sense of who Mark was; as time went on, I realized his story begged to be told, and I had the best shot to tell it. You will soon be the judge of that.

CHAPTER 1

• • •

Fall in Austin, TX is always hot and humid, but on September 16, 2013, it seemed unseasonably so. My grandkids, Tabor and Marshall, were nine and seven. My daughter Nancy and I had walked over to meet them after school. Squeak of backpacks, jingle of those crazy bangles kids hang on them. Hot and sweaty. The kids already knew that their father Mark had gone to the hospital early that morning. They had yet to find out why.

Their dad going to the hospital was not exactly scary to either of them. They knew their father often "had the flu," went to the doctor, came home, and then went back to work. Had been doing that since before they were born, according to Mom and Dad. No big deal. As we walked, they chatted. I stayed silent, knowing this time would be different. It was not my tale to tell.

"Is Daddy going to be OK, Mama?" asked Tabor.

"He's working very hard to get better, but he's really, really sick."

"He's not going to die, is he? He doesn't have cancer, does he?" Tabor's eyes were huge with fear. Marshall started to cry.

"Well…" Nancy hesitated. Tabor stomped to the house. Marshall cried louder, then shouted, "This can be so bad!"

Understatement of the year. Their father, Mark Clifton, 40 years old, did, indeed, have cancer. And he was dying.

• • •

CHAPTER 2

NOVEMBER 1998

I HAD JUST MET TWENTY-SIX-YEAR-OLD Mark Clifton when Nancy brought him to my office to get a tetanus shot for a trip to Machu Picchu. I'm a family physician and was practicing in Dallas at the time. I had heard Mark's name but little else about him from Nancy. They had had a few dates; that's all.

Mark's and Nancy's paths had first crossed in late 1997, when Nancy transferred from Atlanta to Dallas while working for Arthur Andersen. By then Mark was working at the Dallas Andersen office and noted this potential new hire, Nancy Werner, as she was being shown around the office. Nancy says she didn't see him, but he saw her as he sneaked a peek over his cube wall. Hmmm. Later they eyed each other in an elevator, but Mark was dating someone else. Something clicked, though, and in March of 1998 the two of them got together.

Given their relationship, it was natural that my daughter would bring Mark to see me for such a minor need. In the exam room, I treated him like any other patient. Vital signs normal, medical history negative, like most of the young men who had grown up in my practice.

As I examined him briefly, it was obvious he was healthy. His last medical exam had been for a tetanus booster when he was fourteen. I was impressed with this 6'3" slender, soft-spoken, young man with an easy smile and bright blue eyes. He was a college graduate, handsome and comfortable in his skin, just the sort of man Nancy would be dating. My initial thought was: I like this guy.

I was curious about the purpose of his Machu Picchu trip, so I asked him. He answered that he was taking his dad to revisit the place where he, Mark, had been conceived. I didn't get it.

"So, what is the purpose, again?"

"None. I just thought it'd be a fun thing to do."

His exam was certainly normal and was over in a few minutes. My nurse gave him the vaccine, and Mark, Nancy and I went for a sandwich to a little tea shop nearby. I apologized for the girly atmosphere; he laughed, saying there was a little "sissy" café his family visited a lot in Paint Rock. It had the best food in town. He could do sissy, he'd said. I thought to myself, *This is one guy who is very easy to like.* His mother's ancestors were pioneers in Paint Rock, and the ranch remained in the family. In fact, his father Wade had moved out there from Austin about a decade ago, serving as president of the tiny Paint Rock State Bank. His mom Elaine remained in their Austin home to be close to her growing family, now numbering six grandchildren, with much travelling by both Wade and Elaine between the two towns.

As 1998 came to an end, Mark's name slipped into Nancy's vocabulary more often, finally becoming a permanent fixture as they grew closer. He even began to show up at family get-togethers with my other daughter Carol and her family, who at that time also lived in the Dallas area. We all liked him; he had a great sense of humor, was self-deprecating, and enjoyed Carol's two preschool-aged kids. Most of all, he seemed to be totally smitten with Nancy.

It was on a ski trip that Mark told Nancy he had found a lump in his testicle. He had gotten on the internet to research testicular masses, reading all about Lance Armstrong, then a recent testicular cancer victim, from Mark's hometown. It was scary; Mark knew he had to address this quickly.

"Your mom is my doctor. What should I do?" She told him to ask me, of course.

Because of the private nature of testicular exams, I referred him to my favorite urologist, Allan Van Horn, instead of examining him myself. In retrospect, I would have gotten Mark seen immediately had I known how very abnormal his exam would be.

CHAPTER 3

• • •

MAY 1999

OFF THEY WENT TO AN early morning appointment to Dr. Allan Van Horn, just two floors down from my office. Less than an hour into Mark and Nancy's visit, Allan called me.

"I've ordered a sono, Judy; that testis feels like solid cancer."

I knew Allan; he was not an alarmist. He got a STAT testicular sonogram at our hospital, Charlton Methodist. Because of his high index of suspicion, Allan consulted immediately with the radiologist and then called me. Sure enough, the entire testicle looked replaced with cancer. He asked how I wanted the bad news to be delivered.

"Send them back upstairs. I think it will be easier for everyone if I tell them. What's the next step?"

"It has to come off—today. The entire testicle. I've already scheduled Mark as a *to-follow* on today's surgery schedule. Tell him not to eat or drink, starting now."

We stood alone in my office, just Nancy, Mark, and me; by now, it was lunchtime; the office was empty. I told them what Allan had said. Nancy said nothing, just looked at me, her face full of emotion but each of us unable to sort it all out at that point. Mark did not hesitate. He put his arm around Nancy, looked her in the eye, and said, "I'm so sorry."

Not one word of self-pity, not one word of *Why me?* He cared only for what this meant to my daughter. Although he didn't know it at the time, this scenario would replay over and over again as the years went on.

CHAPTER 4

• • •

WITHIN HOURS, MARK'S MOM DROVE from Austin to Dallas; his dad, from Paint Rock. By then it was early evening, and Mark was still waiting for a slot in the busy surgery schedule. He was hungry and thirsty; yet we stood there with water bottles in our hands. After introductions, the three of us talked outside Mark's hospital room while Nancy stayed at his side.

It was our first meeting. I could see the genetics: Mark had his mom's thin structure and quick, broad smile; he had his dad's height and quiet intelligence. Both parents had twinkling blue eyes, explaining Mark's own. As I outlined what I knew up to that point, they quietly got to work dealing with the situation. Calls went out to their two daughters and their families, all of whom lived in Austin.

I sensed the pain the senior Cliftons were feeling. They had each driven for hours; I had the home-court advantage of being in my own hospital, and my patient was under the care of a urologist I trusted. *How much more difficult for them*, I thought.

As we waited, we traded some stories about our children. Elaine told me that while Mark was in kindergarten, his teacher approached her, asking if he had some "kidney issues."

Completely taken aback, Elaine had replied, "No, why?"

"Well, he spends an awful lot of time in the bathroom."

Puzzled, that evening Elaine questioned her son; Mark explained that he was bored, so he was in there reading. I laughed in acknowledgement. Nancy was a reader, too. At our library in Peoria, Illinois, kindergartener

Nancy would check out ten books and read them in the car; by the time we got home, she would have already finished them and wanted to exchange them.

The wait to get "added on" to the surgery schedule continued to drag on for hours. It was a long time for Mark to be without food or drink, but he didn't complain. The nurses on the floor adored him. Here was a young, healthy, and charming guy, cooperative and requiring virtually nothing from them except routine vital signs. They were used to much older, complicated, sickly patients. On East Tower 2, one of his nurses would eventually become his personal cheerleader, following him closely for years to come. But we didn't know that yet.

Finally, at 9:00 p.m., it was Mark's turn in the operating room. We had run out of small talk, and Mark was anxious to get it over with. The surgery was uncomplicated and thus quick. Mark lost his entire left testicle and a few groin lymph nodes. I was so grateful to Allan for doing what he felt needed to be done, despite being so tired at the end of an already long day. The frozen pathological specimen came back as expected: testicular cancer. Later testing referred to it as a non-seminoma, which is the typical young man's testicular cancer and is seen most often in the teens and twenties. Non-seminomas tend to grow and spread quickly.

"He'll want to donate sperm soon since he'll need chemo," Allan told us later in the surgery waiting room. "He's young and healthy and should do well."

Allan had done blood work on Mark that would be back in a few days. He was checking a tumor marker, AFP or *alpha fetal protein*, in particular. This marker is non-specific, but serves as a benchmark for testicular cancer tracking. Normal is less than 4. Mark's turned out to be over 300; it plunged quickly post-op and seven days later, it was nearly normal. He also had to have CT scans of both his chest and abdomen to look for any evidence of the cancer's spread, or metastasis. CT scans are X-rays taken in 360 degrees, then reconfigured by computer to show cross section images of the body. Mark's CT scans were clear.

Back on East Tower 2, Mark was coddled by one and all; he was discharged the next day because overall, he was healthy. I suggested he see Dr. Kathy Arrambide at once; she was an oncologist colleague whom I felt would match his and Nancy's personalities. I had frequently consulted with her and trusted her implicitly. She had an aura of mischief, a quicksilver sense of humor yet was always at the top of her game when it came to cancer treatment. I knew all three of them would become soulmates.

It was an instant fit. Kathy took charge immediately, consulting not just in Dallas, but discussing Mark's case with the nationwide guru of testicular cancer, Dr. Lawrence Einhorn, based in Indianapolis. As always, she spoke in clipped tones, softened by her characteristically quiet and soothing voice.

"First, donate sperm. Then, chemo." Mark rolled his eyes, never having been asked to do either before.

June 1999, about one week post-op, found Mark in a hospital bed at Methodist Dallas Medical Center in downtown Dallas, preparing for his first chemo treatment. I had done my residency training there in the '80s, referring to it as "Mother Methodist." In contrast, Charlton was smaller and newer. But since Kathy's office was currently at "Mother's," that's where she sent Mark. He smiled and laughed when I walked into his hospital room.

"This is no big deal so far, if I don't dwell on this bag full of poison dripping into my arm."

As a twenty-six-year-old who planned to marry (probably my daughter), he had already donated sperm after his surgery at Charlton. After the final IV bag of chemo came to an end, he and Nancy both felt somewhat smug; all the horror stories they had heard about chemo had not affected Mark at all. Then Dr. Arrambide spoke up.

"Now for more chemo in my new office at Charlton." *Oh, that.*

Dr. Arrambide was at that time moving into Charlton's professional building. She was a talented oncologist, but like most doctors in the 1990s, she was not a whiz at computer installation. So, during some early office chemo sessions, Mark helped her set up her computer system and get it running. No surprise here; he had worked with computers since the age of fifteen.

CHAPTER 5

• • •

IN THE 1980s, MARK'S FATHER Wade bought a TI994A computer. Then he taught himself how to use it. He told Mark that he felt computers would be important in the future and that Mark, too, should become familiar with them. So, Mark played around with this strange machine, got comfortable with it, and then taught himself BASIC, or Beginner's All-purpose Symbolic Instruction Coder. At age fifteen, he was even able to program music through a tape recorder. One of Wade's other suggestions nudged Mark, "Never get used to sitting around." So, he took a job at a restaurant showing customers where to park. Not intellectually stimulating, but a good first job for a teen.

A few years later, Wade helped Mark get a job at The Computer Doctor, an electronics repair shop. Mark, then eighteen, first just carried the bulky computers back to the work area. As time went on, Mark recalls, he enjoyed shadowing Bently, the shop's computer technician. His earliest memory was learning about the differences between various power cables.

"There aren't any. They're all the same. But I didn't know that at the time. I just watched Bently and learned a lot just by doing." Soon, computers became an integral part of Mark's milieu.

It came as no surprise, then, that later, to pay his way through college at the University of Texas, he applied for and became the first Austin intern at Apple Computer. After graduation from UT in 1997, he moved to Dallas and took a job at the now-defunct Arthur Andersen, where he served as a computer consultant, and, more importantly, where he first laid eyes on Nancy Werner.

CHAPTER 6

• • •

JUNE 1999

IN THE BEGINNING OF MARK'S office chemo, he felt normal; it was quite easy for him to help Dr. Arrambide, but as chemo continued for weeks, his energy and stamina lagged, and he became more confined to the chairs in the infusion room. Along with nausea and generalized weakness and discomfort, Mark was plagued with hair loss, chills, and diarrhea...the usual devastating combination associated with chemotherapy. He doesn't remember much about all that now...he just recalls being cold all the time and frequenting the bathroom from all the IV fluids pumped into him during the infusions.

When he could no longer help with Dr. Arrambide's electronics, he and Nancy looked through Nancy's old family albums, watched videos on tape, and talked for hours about their situation as a couple. Even though it was a typical sweltering Dallas summer, I found him a comfy knitted "chemo blanket" hoping that he would never have to use it again.

Mark felt cold even walking into stores where cooled air blew down from ceiling vents. His hair had started to fall out in handfuls. Eventually he just shaved it all off. He had never felt the chill on his head when he had hair. Baldness was a new concept.

What did the future hold for Mark and Nancy? As parents, we welcomed each other's kids; our families instantly seemed to accept one another. Thrown together unexpectedly as we were, we leaned on each other. When Elaine moved into the dining room of Mark's apartment, I lent her a bed. Elaine would prepare meals for all of us as Mark started to feel better. It was obvious the two families were comfortable together.

Nancy loved Mark, he loved her, and they both wanted to have children someday; they were both in their late 20s: what if, despite his sperm bank donation, they couldn't have kids? Would she love him anyway? How would he feel if they couldn't conceive? What would it do to their relationship? Round and round they dissected the issue. Mark had not even yet officially asked Nancy to marry him. No amount of discussion could answer their questions about what his doctors referred to as future fertility.

As the weeks of chemo wore on, Dr. Arrambide's treatment became wickedly effective. He was in and out of the bathroom most of the day. He became weak and dehydrated, barely able to get around in his small apartment. At first just an annoyance, this became painful, requiring a gastroenterologist to intervene. No pathology was found, and slowly, slowly, his symptoms abated.

Mark looked so very different after he shaved his head. In the late 1990s only African Americans shaved their heads for fashion. Mark's billiard ball baldness caused many stares; that didn't bother him; the cold air on his scalp certainly did, but he chose not to wear a cap or a wig. One time at the beach, he walked by an African American family; their arms were full of beach toy paraphernalia, and the father looked at Mark and said,

"Hey, brother, can you hold the baby while I get a better grip on things?"

Mark smiled, agreed, took the little boy in his arms, and was rewarded with a big smile from the whole family. As he related the story he marveled that he had found a silver lining in the whole cancer/chemo thing.

"If I'd had a normal haircut, he never would've asked me for help."

The term peach fuzz had a whole new meaning for Mark. Elaine took a picture of him clowning with a peach balanced on his shining head. I can still recall him several months later in my kitchen in Cedar Hill when his hair was barely sprouting. Raising his hand to his face, he blew as hard as he could on his thumb, like he was blowing up a balloon.

"I'm trying to make it grow even faster. See? It's working!"

Despite normal AFP, Mark and Nancy continued to struggle with the whole concept of cancer at such a young age. Dr. Arrambide continued to consult via phone with Dr. Einhorn, who agreed with her treatment and opinions; he too felt that only surveillance was necessary at that point. Mark would have AFP bloodwork and CT scans of chest and abdomen on a repeating six-month basis.

Several months before Mark and Nancy had known about his cancer, they had planned a trip to Cancun for later in 1999. After surgery and chemo, follow-up visits with Dr. Arrambide had been uneventful, so Mark asked her about whether he was safe to go. Kathy, after some thought, agreed that if Mark would stay hydrated, wear sunscreen, and avoid alcohol, she would OK the trip.

Mark was ecstatic, but Nancy refused to go. Mark, surprised, insisted; he didn't want to spoil it for her, and he agreed to abide by any guidelines Kathy had set up. But Nancy had a different agenda.

"If we get there, and you get sick, I won't know how to take care of you."

He argued valiantly but finally had to give in, knowing she was correct. Little did they know that someday she would take care of him for months on end; in fact, in years to come, Mark's future doctors would frequently credit Nancy with saving his life.

Instead of going to Cancun, the couple began to plan their future together. They did reach a conclusion about their relationship; Nancy realized her love for Mark was greater than her fear of never having a child. He knew that she was "the one" for him. They had made it through surgery and eight weeks of chemo; now they were ready to get on with their lives together.

In the meantime, Arthur Andersen went out of business, and they both needed a job. Neither was committed to living in Dallas. A computer wizard and Austin native, Mark's decision was an easy one. He interviewed at Dell in Austin and was hired as an intern that fall. Nancy liked Austin, too. Easy decision for her too; in August, they moved there and lived with Mark's parents. Shortly thereafter, Nancy also became a Dell employee. Elaine helped them house hunt, and in December the young couple closed on and prepared to move into their new home on Grapevine Lane.

One year later, they added their first dog, a newly weaned Cavalier King Charles. He was an instant hit with all the family. My son Tom was there at Christmas when the pup was just a brown and white fur ball. Initially Mark and Nancy planned to name him Rowdy, but he just didn't look like a Rowdy. At one point, Tom picked him up and said,

"You look like a Baxter."

Yes! This dog had presence. He was the alpha, or so he seemed to consider himself. Thus, he became and remained Baxter. He was the focal point of their Christmas picture that year. Eventually they had him trained as a therapy dog, and the three of them visited nursing homes and hospitals. They had a painting made of him dressed in a leather jacket, paw up, looking cool. That painting still hangs in the dining room. I can't help smiling every time I see it. Baxter lived for fifteen years.

Both back at work at Dell, Mark bought Nancy a ring and formally proposed; she accepted, and on May 12, 2001, they were married on the beach in Saint John, Virgin Islands. Family and a few dear friends attended; at their reception back in Austin, Mark and Nancy announced they planned to be pregnant by their first anniversary.

• • •

CHAPTER 7

Fall 2001

Despite normal AFPs, Mark's chest CT scan showed some unusual tissue in his anterior mediastinum. This is an area just behind the breastbone. Although fibrous, it is basically hollow in nature. It is like a closet stretching from the breastbone in the front (anterior) all the way to the vertebrae in the back (posterior). Coursing through this small area are important structures like the heart, aorta and other large vessels, trachea, and esophagus.

Mark's abnormality, luckily, was very much in the front or anterior aspect, just behind the top of the breastbone; thus, he underwent a mediastinoscopy at an outpatient surgery center in Austin. This involved making a small slit at the top of the breastbone, inserting a tiny endoscope and looking around in that area.

A small amount of tissue was found, biopsied, and sent to the lab for a frozen section. I was in a hospital meeting when Nancy called me afterwards; I stepped out, wanting to know the results but also afraid to find out. *Hooray!* The tissue was a benign or non-malignant teratoma.

While benign is good, a teratoma is bad for a testicular cancer survivor. By definition, a teratoma is a germ cell tumor, normally occurring inside the testis in a male. Incompletely understood, a male teratoma can also occur outside the testis; this is uncommon, but when it does occur, the mediastinum is not an unusual place to find it. Although there was no way to be sure, a question lingered: *Could this unusual small benign mediastinal germ cell tumor come back later to haunt Mark as a malignancy, since he'd already had testicular cancer?* There was no way to tell for sure.

Mark concentrated on the word benign and went home from the surgery center with just a Band-Aid low on his neck; the next day, he went back to work. Nancy did too. Life was going along well, despite an occasional issue like this. They assumed this was merely a speed bump in Mark's cancer saga. They were wrong.

CHAPTER 8

• • •

IN LATE NOVEMBER 2001, MARK's routine CT scan picked up another abnormality. A bigger mass was found in his left chest. Dr. Arrambide felt the time had come for Mark to consult face-to-face with testicular cancer guru, Dr. Einhorn. She asked me to have the films sent STAT. This was easy; by the end of the day, the task was done.

Sending films was easy; receiving them during the holidays was not. Back then, there was no ability to transmit images electronically from one hospital to another. After many maddening phone calls and rerouting, the CT films finally arrived on Dr. Einhorn's desk. He agreed it was time to consult on his campus, both with him and his choice of cardiothoracic surgeons, Dr. Kenneth Kesler. Before Mark's diagnosis in 1999, we had never heard of these two doctors. Soon, however, both their names would be engraved forever on our memories.

We had heard early on from Dr. Kathy Arrambide that Dr. Einhorn was considered the wizard of testicular cancer treatment in America, so we accepted that Mark would be in good hands. Later, we would learn that this was an oversimplification. In 2016, Dr. Einhorn was named as one of the "Fifty Most Influential Physicians in History" by Medscape, a medical online website for physicians. Other physicians included in the distinction were Hippocrates, Freud, and Papanicolaou (who pioneered the Pap smear), to name a few. Very impressive company indeed.

So far, cancer and its never-ending threat had intruded into Mark's and Nancy's lives far too many times. They talked about its effect on their future children, deciding then and there never to reveal Mark's diagnosis to their kids. They wanted a family that was happy, healthy, and normal. They felt they were exactly that. I recall Mark sitting at their kitchen table, eating breakfast. He was waxing eloquent about how great his life was. Then he paused and added, "Ya know, if it weren't for this stupid cancer, life would be perfect."

He was not aware at the time that he had coined the term "stupid cancer." It would come back to haunt him someday.

With that in mind, Mark and Nancy flew to Indiana. They met with Drs. Einhorn and Kesler, both of whom agreed the mass needed to come out. They found themselves about to face another surgery. The significance and origin of the mass was unknown, but the decision to proceed with surgery in a few weeks was made; after returning to Austin, they contacted me and Mark's parents: Would we go with them for the surgery?

CHAPTER 9

• • •

THE FIRST WEEK OF DECEMBER 2001, found all five of us in Indianapolis. I was wearing an American flag pin, given to me by a patient after 9/11, on my sweater. That tragedy was still prominent on America's newscasts, and the usual pre-Christmas hype seemed much subdued. In fact, Nancy noted that Mark's surgery was to be on Pearl Harbor Day, December 7. It was an unhappy time for us all, as a family and as a nation.

Dinner the night before surgery went quietly; we all had little to say. Because space was limited, we all shared a room at Hope Lodge a few miles from IUPUI Hospital—Indiana University/Purdue University in Indianapolis. Hope Lodge, run by the American Cancer Society, offers free housing for cancer patients and their families while they are hospitalized.

Nancy told us the next morning that Mark had gotten up in the middle of the night to look out the window and beat his chest Tarzan-style. I asked why he did that; his answer, with Mark's typical grin, "Because I could; after surgery, I won't be able to."

In the cold early morning dark of the next day, we arrived at the IUPUI. As soon as we walked in, I was impressed with the hospital. First, signage was clear, thus comforting. That may sound strange, but hospitals are seen by visitors as foreign and frightening; anything to soften that impression is welcome. At IUPUI, each corridor was marked with an old-fashioned street sign showing the way. It felt like we were part of a community, not in some huge place sure to be full of serious illness. Little bistros scattered throughout the hospital were creature comforts for times when the main cafeteria was closed.

Mark was very upbeat as he was taken to the preoperative area or pre-op. He smiled and joked as usual; Nancy worried but tried not to show it. Surgical fellow Dr. Brian Kogon, who was near Mark's age, had gone over all the paperwork with them, answering last-minute questions. As a fellow, he had already graduated both from medical school and his surgical residency and was now studying the subspecialty of cardiothoracic surgery. He would assist Dr. Kesler in the OR. Cellphone cameras were a thing of the future, so we have no pictures from our time in the preop area.

Finally, the moment came for Mark to be taken back. After kisses and hugs for good luck, he disappeared behind the massive double doors to the OR. The four of us settled into the surgical waiting room. We were given nametags with Mark's name on them to streamline the flow of information. Nancy had brought her laptop to watch movies but had a hard time concentrating. Wade and Elaine murmured comforting memories. Many trips were made to get coffee and snacks. Heavy sighs were heard from all of us.

After what seemed an eternity, we heard Mark's name called out by the OR messenger. She told us with a smile that the surgical team had "cracked" Mark's chest open by sawing down through the breastbone, spreading it open, to remove the mass; Mark was doing well. However, Dr. Kesler wanted to go further. He wanted to turn Mark onto his right side and do a surgery called a clamshell procedure on the left side of his chest. This would involve prying apart the left outer ribs to get a closer view of the remains of the mass to be sure it was entirely removed. Was Nancy OK with that?

How do you answer that? Certainly! If that's needed, do it! But the fact that it was a longer, more invasive surgery and rather gruesome-sounding, was also unsettling. I noticed that even the always positive and unruffled Wade had tears in his eyes.

Once again, the hours crawled on. The messenger updated us regularly that all was well, and, finally, Mark was sent to ICU post-op. Dr. Kesler, a man of few words, felt everything was fine. So, we did too.

When I first saw Mark later that day, his hospital gown was gone and suctioning chest tubes protruded from both left and middle chest. Several kinds of IVs snaked into multiple veins. Huge bandages swathed his torso from chin to navel. I recall thinking, as I looked at his long thin body sprawled in the bed, that he looked like Christ crucified. He was not in pain while lying quietly, but any movement to sit or stand was excruciating that first day.

As in past surgeries, Mark progressed well. In a few days, the pathological report came back as a benign teratoma. There was that unusual tumor again, but this time in a harder-to-reach place, requiring serious surgery. Because non-malignant tumors require no chemotherapy, after this surgery, Mark just returned back to surveillance as in the past: checking AFP levels, and repeating CT scans regularly.

I made out my Christmas cards during the long hours spent in the ICU waiting room. Nancy read funny articles to Mark to help pass the time. Although he progressed well, there were some scary issues with his heart monitor tracings, but a complete cardiac workup ruled out any damage. The surgeons felt that all the manipulations to remove the mass had irritated the pericardium, the sac the heart sits in. It would heal on its own, and no medicine would be needed. In just a few days, Mark was transferred to a step-down unit, where he met his roommate and fellow testicular cancer patient, Hoss, from Mississippi.

Never were there two more unlike roommates. Hoss's feeling about testicular cancer was that it was a sort of profanity, a life-threatening menace that came out of nowhere and required unthinkable medicines and humiliating surgeries to be rained upon him. His approach was to avoid talking about it, even to his doctors, but he admitted to Mark that he wondered about it just the same. He asked Mark for any insight, and Mark gladly shared his knowledge, explaining that there was no way to predict or prevent testicular cancer and no better way to treat it than surgery. Over time, Hoss relaxed a bit.

They formed a sort of loosely-held bond that continued for years, even into 2005 when Hurricane Katrina caused them to lose contact for a while. Hoss's wife Shandra still trades emails with Nancy.

While Mark recuperated, we returned to Hope Lodge. It was actually a renovated motel. Since it was the holiday season, the place was decorated to the rafters. There were no televisions in guest rooms; patients' families were encouraged to interact, not to hole up and worry about the treatments at the hospital.

There were free laundry facilities and plenty of extra supplies purposely left by those who had come before. A treadmill with a TV encouraged needed exercise for us, grounded as we were for hours at the hospital. Cleaning supplies and equipment were plentiful. We bought toilet tissue, a new shower curtain, and bathroom throw rugs; when we checked out, we followed tradition and left those items behind. Local businesses had also donated individual packages of shampoo, lip balm, and hand lotion for guests.

A lending library with computer access was there, too; at the time, quite a luxury. Nancy checked in regularly with the pet boarding facility where Baxter was staying. Seeing him real-time on a computer was another new concept we all engaged in and laughed about. Plaques dedicated by families of cancer patients lined the walls. A free shuttle ran regularly to the hospital and back. Hope Lodge was perfectly named; we were grateful for being able to stay, free of charge, at such a trying time. Although rebuilt in a new location, this wonderful service remains in Indianapolis to this day and has been built in other cities as well.

Nancy, Wade, Elaine and I stayed up late in the common area atrium, putting together jigsaw puzzles, drinking hot chocolate, chit-chatting with other patients' families while Mark recuperated in the hospital. The entire common area felt like a cozy chalet. Walls were made of burnished wood, and the cathedral ceiling reflected the light from a huge fireplace at the far wall. An enormous Christmas tree was hung with a multitude of decorations, many of them handmade. A cheery electric train ran in a circle under the tree. Here and there were recliners and love seats. This, indeed, did not feel like a motel; we felt a true sense of camaraderie, of caring, from both staff and other patients' families.

To the right of the common area lay six complete mini-kitchens, each in an open but self-contained cubicle. Every small kitchen was camper-sized, complete with appliances and supplies needed to cook and enjoy a meal anytime night or day. Cabinets lined the outer walls, marked by family name on masking tape on the doors. A family could bring as much or as little as desired. Nobody pilfered. Since some families had to stay for months, these kitchens were a godsend.

One day, coming back tired and hungry to the Lodge from the hospital, we were met by the aroma of barbecue. In the common eating area near the kitchens were several other families, eating together. They waved us over. Serving everyone was the husband of a cancer victim; he had spent weeks at Hope Lodge over the years while she was hospitalized, and she had recently passed away. In her honor, he had personally cooked, then served a holiday dinner for everyone at Hope Lodge; it was obvious he knew all the staff, and his welcome to us strangers was heartfelt. He said that Hope Lodge had been such a haven to him during his wife's long battle with cancer; he was doing this in memory of her.

And what a meal it was! It seemed like we were back in Texas: ribs, chicken, and brisket, rich in spicy barbecue sauce with all the trimmings. Although I don't even recall our host's name, I will forever keep this shared meal in my memory—it was so heartwarming and savory at the same time. The lodge director made the rounds with the husband. We shared a table with Hoss's family: they were quiet and comfortable people; chatting with them was a pleasure, since Mark and Hoss spent their time as roommates healing in the step-down unit. We learned that Hoss's family was from a small town in Mississippi. They had driven the nearly 700 miles to seek IUPUI's cancer care. Conversation was lively, and memories were shared; there were more smiles than tears. It was a lovely tribute.

Over the course of his stay at IUPUI, Mark also became friends with Dr. Brian Kogon, the surgical fellow who had assisted on his case. Although Mark's tumor turned out to be a benign teratoma, its removal had been a real teaching case. The two-part surgery had been complex and difficult; it advanced Dr. Kogon's horizons as a future cardiothoracic surgeon.

Mark and Brian clicked. Both were in their late twenties, bright, and talkative. Brian had scrubbed in on Mark's case and followed it until discharge. He took a personal interest in Mark beyond the usual physician/patient relationship. Even after discharge from IUPUI, their camaraderie extended to Brian's later taking Mark out for wings and beer. Later they went skiing together. Years later, around 2009, Brian and Mark would meet for dinner in Austin. Dr. Kogon eventually completed his cardiothoracic fellowship in Indiana and is now a leading authority of both pediatric and adult congenital heart disease at Emory University in Atlanta. To be skilled enough for a dual subspecialty requires both a rare talent and nearly a decade of postgraduate training.

Post-op, Mark's usual good health served him well. He healed quickly and was discharged from IUPUI in just a few days, then rested a few days with Nancy in Indianapolis after the rest of us had left for Texas. After they returned to the hospital to thank the staff for their great care, they flew back in time to attend the annual Christmas dinner at Wade and Elaine's Austin home.

After the usual huge meal, we took a walk around the neighborhood. I was amazed that Mark would even want to come along; but he did, and I secretly kept an eye on him in case he showed any signs of overexerting himself. He walked slowly, but surely. In fact, only his eighty-year-old grandmother got a bit short of breath as we went, but in true Clifton fashion, she continued on.

CHAPTER 10

• • •

2002

As the New Year was ushered in, we all rejoiced that Mark had dodged yet another cancer bullet, but due to the brutal surgery he still had a bit of recuperation to do. This, of course, did not prevent his going back to work at Dell right away in January.

After his incisions healed, he and Nancy bought a hot tub to help soothe the tight muscles in his chest; this became his favorite means of relaxation. Since his chest had been opened in two places, breathing was initially painful and at first, exercise was out of the question. But, as before, he normalized quickly. He ate right (although, Dell did bake those fresh chocolate chip cookies on campus, and the aroma…). Alcohol was a rarity. Labs were done routinely, and CT scans followed every six months. Everything was well.

Life went merrily on. Mark's medical routine followed his usual drill: have surgery, recuperate quickly, go back to work and get on with life. This time, however, he paid much more attention to his health. His feet were painful and at times, numb. Technically referred to as post-chemo peripheral neuropathy, this was a long-lasting side effect of Mark's IV chemotherapy treatment. He was offered medication to relieve discomfort but preferred just to live with it.

In May, Mark and Nancy celebrated their first wedding anniversary, but without their hoped-for pregnancy. Mark had fully recovered from the massive surgery and was looking ahead. He and Nancy continued at Dell—he as an Executive Briefing Center Consultant, she in Human Resources.

Almost a year later they did, however, add another family member: Beauregard, a Cavalier King Charles, like Baxter. Unlike suave Baxter, Beau was the runt of the litter, deaf, and with eyes that didn't converge. But he was their choice, and his sweet personality more than made up for any physical shortcomings. Baxter, typical alpha, constantly reminded little Beau just what the pecking order was at the Clifton's.

Mark adored these two dogs, and he had selected the type of puppies. Before getting Baxter, he had seen a 'Cav' being walked by its owner and told Nancy, "That's the dog I want."

After Baxter, he wanted another, so Beau was added to the family.

And why not? They were the typical DINKS (double income no kids), both having had pets as children. They spent hours in obedience training, even leading to Baxter's becoming a therapy dog. Mark always cuddled those dogs, singing to them, teasing them, and playing with them. The two dogs romped and played, sometimes a bit too much. When they were still puppies, they often escaped, despite reinforcing the backyard fence and watching every time the front door opened. Mark became famous in his neighborhood for his performance early one Saturday morning. He had opened the front door to get the newspaper when Baxter shot out. Still dressed in his boxers, Mark chased Baxter down the street, hollering after his pet. Witnessing this was Shirley Hooper, their longtime neighbor and friend; she's never let him forget what a hilarious scene that was.

CHAPTER 11

• • •

SUMMER 2003

AFTER BEAU ARRIVED, NANCY AND Mark started to think about adding some two-legged members to the family. They chose not to use Mark's sperm donated in 1999; they wanted a natural initiation of parenthood. They joked about sperm storage fees, referring to them as "paying rent on the kids."

I was working in the ER when I got a call from Nancy.

"We're pregnant!"

Nancy sailed through pregnancy and continued to work. When she and Mark went to her OB's office for a sonogram, they asked the technician not to reveal the baby's gender. Instead, the technician sealed the news into an envelope. Shortly thereafter, Mark took Nancy on a trip to DC, where they opened the envelope to find they were having a girl.

"Tabor!" Nancy had liked the name for years, having heard it while in college; it would be fine for either a boy or a girl, but seemed more apt for a girl.

Nancy and Mark were ecstatic—it was an exciting time of continuing to work, painting the nursery, buying baby furniture and being honored at a shower. Mark maintained his vigilance of being cancer-tested, each time being assured that he was fine.

There were minor ups and downs in his labs that often went unexplained—a supreme annoyance for both Nancy and Mark. Oncologist

Dr. Einhorn in Indiana and Mark's Austin oncologist, Dr. Jerry Fain, reviewed the labs and repeated the same mantra: since Mark had no symptoms, only surveillance was needed; he was to keep doing the routine blood work and CT scans. But the thought was omnipresent, no matter how hard he tried to ignore it: *what if the cancer comes back?*

On April 6, 2004, during a drenching downpour, I sat in gridlocked traffic on the way to the hospital; this time, a happy event. Mark called me from the delivery room and I could hear Tabor's early cries over my mobile phone.

"They're beautiful!" was all Mark could say. "Nancy and Tabor are fine."

As usual with a firstborn in the family, they took oodles of pictures of Tabor; she was understandably the spotlight of their lives. The couple decided that Nancy would remain at home rather than go back to Dell. It was clear to them that raising their child would be more important than a second paycheck.

A newborn always changes the family dynamics. Mark was now thirty-two; despite the benign teratoma surgery in 2001, he remained cancer-free and had been since the original nonseminoma in 1999. So, he and Nancy, also in her thirties, began to make plans to complete their family. No real need, though: Nancy was already two months pregnant.

On October 27, 2005, Marshall Thomas Clifton came into the world. He was healthy and vigorous. Once again, it was a time of great rejoicing and a lot of work. In no uncertain terms, they had their hands full. When Nancy and Mark brought Marshall home, Tabor was eighteen months old; they realized this was going to be a huge undertaking: two in diapers, two in cribs, and two in car seats. Initially, Tabor couldn't pronounce Marshall's name; she called him "Baby" for months.

The next two years were a blur…the house on Grapevine Lane overflowed with mountains of laundry, feeding schedules and baby paraphernalia. Fatigue from two tiny kids brought the usual challenges: lack of sleep, doctor visits, and "What's for dinner?" Mark and Nancy agreed their most important duty as parents was: *be there*. Mark passed up travel and promotion opportunities at Dell to assure being home by six o'clock. He took an active part in raising his family and stuck close to home. Nancy did not return to her job. Life was hectic but normal for a young, growing family.

• • •

CHAPTER 12

MARCH 2007

MORE THAN FIVE YEARS HAD passed, post-diagnosis, without a recurrence of Mark's cancer. Mark was pronounced cured. Nancy planned a surprise celebration with family and friends at Iron Cactus, their favorite restaurant. Snapshots from the evening confirm that Mark was overwhelmed with the huge turnout. Afterward, Nancy had the party invitation framed along with a picture taken that evening. It still hangs in their dining room.

I took the children to the party, but left with them early since they were only two and three years old at the time. I recall Tabor saying, "But Nana, we didn't get any birthday cake." In her opinion, if there was a party, it had to be a birthday party.

With two toddlers, both Nancy and Mark had their hands full as parents, but everyone was doing well. Life seemed to be progressing. There are pictures taken of the four of them, even tiny Marshall, participating in a Livestrong marathon supporting cancer research. Thanksgiving trips to the family ranch with the rest of the Clifton clan were a tradition. The four of them wearing red plaid Christmas pajamas was another. In 2009, Mark began a tradition of creating a calendar for each of us in the family; he spent hours on the computer, compiling family pictures taken over the previous year, presenting the finished product as Christmas gifts for the family. Mine hung in my office over my desk; it was my daily touchstone of good memories. I have kept every calendar, for each year documents the memories of a thriving family.

Reading to the kids at night and snuggling with them before tucking them in became routine for both parents. Not that it always worked out perfectly, but life spooled on in a predictable fashion. There were the usual challenges of teething, potty training, and the first days of school. The decision that the children were never to know Mark had cancer remained intact, and the *C-word* was not mentioned. Still, the thought of cancer never left Mark's radar.

If you have ever talked to a cancer survivor, you become aware of the constant fear of cancer recurrence. The survivor keeps looking over his shoulder, just in case. It is a life of scrutinizing any little symptom, wondering if there is some hint that once a victim, you must endure the horror all over again. It is like a much-focused phobia, a finely-honed post-traumatic stress disorder (or PTSD) that forever hovers. Every cough, every sniffle can set off the thought *"What if...?"* Mark went through this, too; he would call me at times for advice about certain symptoms, unsure if they were part of some ominous pattern. Except for a few bouts of allergy problems, he remained healthy.

CHAPTER 13

• • •

BETWEEN 2007 AND 2009, MARK quietly tracked his AFP and did his CT scans as recommended. The scans remained normal. The AFP, however, at times veered into the abnormal zone, just enough to heighten concern for recurrence, but never enough for either Dr. Einhorn or Dr. Fain to justify intervention. Mark had no symptoms; his CT scans remained normal. Both doctors recommended continuing surveillance.

Watching and waiting is one of the hardest tasks for both patient and doctor. The *what if* syndrome is impossible to evade for the patient. For the doctor, the same mental argument occurs, but from a different perspective: the AFP increases were so minimal that to intervene would be premature and without a goal. The Hippocratic Oath clearly states, "First, do no harm." Doing anything, especially when unnecessary, causes more problems than it solves. Thus, to intervene without a sound reason is not practicing good medicine.

Still, doctors are trained to act quickly; telling a doctor to wait is like telling the sunrise to wait. When the AFP levels no longer merely fluctuated but began to climb steadily in the spring of 2010, Mark and Nancy made the trip to Indiana to visit Dr. Einhorn. Did he suspect a recurrence of Mark's cancer?

He did, and Nancy and Mark agreed with his recommended course of action. The good news was that the surgery could safely be done nonemergently in Austin; the bad news was that Mark would now also lose his entire right testicle. This meant that at the age of thirty-eight, his body would require testosterone shots.

The tissue type this time was a seminoma, rather than the nonseminoma of his previous left testicular cancer. Having both tissue types of testicular cancer is rare. Both cancers require chemotherapy treatment, though. Because of the side effect of the two different IV chemo treatments he had received, even though years apart, Mark would be unable ever to undergo such treatment again. We hoped he'd never have to face that.

After healing from having the orchiectomy, or removal of the testicle, Mark first squeezed in his chemo treatments around his work schedule. The familiar drill of frequent rounds of chemo during the day began. But, as before, he became weak, lost his hair and fought constant digestive symptoms.

Finally the last dose was in sight, but it ended up being scheduled on Memorial Day, and the infusion office was closed; it turned out to be an entire day's ordeal just to find a place to finish his chemo. I stayed with Tabor and Marshall.

Both Mark and Nancy looked worn-out when they arrived home. It was nearly evening. Four-year-old Marshall crawled on the couch where Mark sagged, thin, haggard, and pale, eyes closed.

"I wish you weren't sick, Daddy," he said.

"Me too, Buddy," was all Mark could manage. The next morning, Mark got up and went back to work. Again.

CHAPTER 14

• • •

LIFE RETURNED SLOWLY TO NORMAL. Tabor began first grade in the fall of 2010 at Davis Elementary, a public school just minutes from the house. Marshall was in pre-K at a more distant school. This entailed much driving about for Nancy, as she took an active part in the kids' lives. Mark continued to do well and regained his strength. Routine household chores and the kids' activities kept Nancy busy.

Pictures from my son's Los Angeles wedding in August show a nearly-bald Mark, smiling into the camera with his family. Mark and Nancy enjoyed getting away for a few days and flew the family out for the festivities. Both Tabor and Marshall were in the ceremony, giving them all a reason to dress up. If Mark had had a full head of hair, he would have appeared totally normal.

Time marched on. From 2011 to early 2013, Mark quietly continued his surveillance of his labs and imaging, saving the data on his computer. He didn't discuss his AFP not returning to normal the way it had before. Reviewing his data with Dr. Einhorn by phone, Mark was advised, as before, to continue getting twice-yearly labs and CT scans. He did so religiously; there were no huge upswings in the AFP, and he felt fine, but that cancer survivor reflex was always tickling at the back of his brain.

In 2011, Mark felt well enough to do an exercise boot camp; this is amazing for anyone with neuropathy in his feet. But it was typical Mark not to back away from any challenge. Later that year, in the shower one night, he found a thickening on his chest wall. His instant thought was, *"Is this a recurrence?"* So off he and Nancy went for a biopsy.

Thankfully, the results were just fatty tissue; Mark continued his usual routine, working long hours, progressing well in his career. In 2012, he was named Global Solutions Marketing Director of Cloud Strategy for this new concept called *The Cloud*. He even began to do a bit of short-term travelling once the kids were in the same school all day: Las Vegas, New York, and even China. Mark was the "go-to" guy, and we watched YouTube videos of his presentations; on camera, he was relaxed and obviously having fun doing his job, despite its incredible complexity.

Mark and the family were happy; things were going along well. In late spring of 2013, he took the business trip to China, returning shortly before our entire family, thirteen of us, planned a vacation week in York, Maine. Mark took a hard look at his AFP: the value had crept up to over 200 again although his CT scans were still normal. Then they weren't.

• • •

CHAPTER 15

MAY 2013

A ROUTINE CHEST CT SHOWED a small tumor in Mark's left chest; it was about the size of a matchbox. It was not the size that was the problem however, it was the location. This mass was wrapped around the three most important structures in his left chest: the thoracic aorta, the left main stem bronchus, and left main pulmonary artery.

A PET scan was performed. PET stands for positron emission tomography; this uses radioactive material to produce a 3-D image. It is used in cancer patients when the cancer has appeared somewhere new, or metastasized. And there it was, constricting those structures.

The left lung is much more crowded than the right because the heart and its attached huge aorta take up so much room in the left chest cavity. Both lungs serve the body by adding oxygen back to deoxygenated blood delivered to them from the right side of the heart.

First, the heart accepts deoxygenated blood on its right side, which is flimsy and thin-walled. The right heart is essentially a collecting bag for dirty blood from the entire body. Think of deoxygenated blood as blue or cyanotic: the color of someone choking. That blood lacks oxygen; in fact, in medical school gross anatomy class, our cadavers' veins had been injected with blue dye and arteries with red, to help differentiate venous versus arterial blood flow.

Compared to the right side of the heart, the lungs represent a low-pressure system, and blood flows there easily from the right heart, almost as if downhill. The blood is quickly reoxygenated and then flows out of the lungs and into the left side of the heart. In contrast to the floppy wall of the right heart, the left heart's wall is very muscular—the workhorse of the entire organ. From there, the freshly reoxygenated blood is pumped directly into the thoracic or chest part of the aorta, and immediately out to the body. The body cannot function for more than a few minutes without oxygen, so if the heart is not pumping correctly, the whole body suffers.

A properly functioning aorta is vital: it is the largest artery in the body and comes directly out of the left ventricle, full of fresh blood. To call the aorta the lifeline of the body is no exaggeration. In an adult male, for example, it is nearly an inch in diameter.

Herein lay Mark's dilemma. Three vital structures in Mark's chest were compromised by this tumor: the huge fresh blood conduit from the heart, the aorta; the huge left lung air conduit, the left main stem bronchus; and one of the two large vessels carrying deoxygenated blood to the lungs, the left main pulmonary artery. The tumor was choking off all three of these essential structures. It was if a tourniquet were intertwined with three of the most important structures in Mark's left chest. The matchbook-sized tumor had far-reaching significance in terms of how surgeons would go about removing it without damaging these nearby vital anatomical structures.

In early June, Mark and Nancy connected by phone to Dr. Einhorn and Dr. Kesler in Indianapolis. After reviewing Mark's data, they did not hesitate: surgery again on Mark's left chest was essential. As soon as a date for the surgical team to handle this complex surgery could be arranged, Mark would be notified. Dr. Kesler planned basically the same operation he had previously performed on Mark: opening the chest through the breastbone and then doing a clamshell procedure to ensure removal of the entire tumor.

The third week of June, my children, their children, my significant other, John, and I—were spending a long-awaited family vacation week in York Harbor, Maine. The thirteen of us played croquet and ersatz games of baseball in the side yard. We boogie boarded in the Atlantic, grilled outdoors, and constructed a huge jigsaw puzzle. The laughter and good-natured teasing were music to my ears.

But it was also during this time that Mark received word about his surgery; it would be in a month, in Indiana with Dr. Kesler. Details were few since the location of the tumor was so precarious; Dr. Kesler was organizing his team and strategizing on just how to approach this small but dangerously-placed mass without damaging any of the vital structures around it. As we were to hear then and many times in the future from his doctors, "We've never been faced with an identical situation; we will do the best we can."

What more could we ask from this elite team of doctors who were not only highly skilled but who also had been familiar with Mark's case for the last twelve years? It seemed a given that this was not going to be as simple as removing a cancerous testis. Nor would it be as simple as his 2001 left chest surgery, even though Dr. Kesler was planning to use the same approach. Mark quizzed him point-blank over the phone.

"Can I survive this surgery?"

"That's my plan."

Mark told us it was not exactly the most confidence-inspiring answer, but it certainly was honest.

The grim news didn't stop Mark's participation in our family revelry in our final days together in Maine, however. He sunbathed on the beach with the rest of us. In the dining room of our rented cottage, we watched a slideshow of Nancy and her brother and sister from the 1980s, and Mark laughed and hooted along with everyone else. Marshall piped up halfway through, "Who are these people?" and brought the house down.

Mark chose not to bring up or go into detail about what awaited him in less than a month. He was on a family vacation; he was going to enjoy it. The entire family went down to the beach one evening. Mark was the designated cameraman, but the rest of us caught him on film clowning around, pretending to be a fashion photographer. It reminded me of Mark at Hope Lodge in 2001, the night before his surgery, pounding on his chest at the window. Always the optimist, always the jokester.

CHAPTER 16

• • •

JULY 2013 ARRIVED ALL TOO soon. Members of both the Werner and Clifton families were in Indianapolis to lend moral support. Nancy posted regular updates and pictures on CaringBridge, a website that enables friends and families to share information about health issues; Mark had chosen the title page,"Stupid Cancer".

Mark was cheered on, both in person and electronically as good wishes poured in from all over. John and I stayed at their home in Austin to provide the children a sense of normalcy. Before they left, Nancy and Mark had reminded us that they had never used the "C-word" in front of the children and asked us to respect their decision, which we did, of course. I was extra careful while logging into CaringBridge.org so Tabor and Marshall could not see Mark's choice of title. The website was a godsend for informing those of us in Austin about what was happening in Indiana at IUPUI. Nancy was the designated author, sending information and pictures as the days unfolded. Friends signed in and sent encouraging words to them both.

There was plenty back in Austin to keep a seven- and nine-year-old busy. John taught both children how to play chess. I taught them Sudoku. They had no idea that cancer had attacked their dad again and exposed him to yet another brutal surgery. They thought Nancy and Mark were on a business trip.

The surgery went well, but was long and tedious. Mark even had to be put on the heart/lung machine during part of it. Adhesions from Mark's 2001 surgery presented the biggest problem.

Adhesions often occur after surgery. They are internal dense fibrous bands that form scar tissue as the body heals itself. Mark's adhesions were thick, tough, and everywhere. I visualize them as a gelatinous mix of unset cement poured all over the inside of the left chest cavity and then left to harden; in Mark's case, for over a decade. Now the task was to remove that old set-up concrete without damaging whatever it was attached to. Doing this with surgical tools inside a human body requires strength, patience, and finesse; too gentle a stroke with the instrument accomplishes frustratingly few results; too hard, and the whole rigid mess can shatter, taking viable body tissue with it.

That was just dealing with the adhesions, merely trying to get an unobstructed view of where the cancer lay and how mixed-in with normal tissue it was. Dr. Kesler and his team found that even the healthy tissues fell apart when they attempted to dissect out the cancer entangled with them. It was like trying to till a rocky field that was more rocks than field. Time after time, the sutures that were so exquisitely put in would lose their grip and need to be replaced. Subsequent bleeding had to be stopped before moving along. It required enormous and unrelenting millimeter-by-millimeter assessment, adjustment, and amazing surgical skill.

The operative report reflected the meticulousness needed and frustration encountered, trying to remove sticky and invasive tumor and adhesion tissue from normal tissues. Dr. Kesler repeatedly used the words "laborious" and "very labor-intensive" to describe his task. Just a few examples of the many difficulties encountered:

"...it became very clear that the significant length of the pulmonary artery involved with this infiltrating mass clearly precluded patch repair."

"...bleeding unfortunately ...could not be repaired despite 2-3 efforts..."

"Further attempts at repair of the aorta failed due to continued bleeding..."

Thus, once the tumor was hacked away from its grip on the aorta, it became obvious to the surgical team that there was not enough aortic tissue left for adequate blood flow, and a large Dacron graft was sewn into place high up in the aorta.

Another downside of this mass was that the cancer had invaded the left lung vessels and airway to the point that the left lung was barely functioning. It was almost completely choked off. Unable to do its job, the entire left lung and its left main pulmonary artery had to be sacrificed. To serve as a protective buffer between the aortic graft and what remained in the left chest, a piece of the pericardium, or the lining of the heart, was used. As I read the operative report, I was in awe: what a masterpiece of surgical skill this represented!

There was other damage, too. The vagus nerve originates in the brain and runs far south into the body. The cancerous mass had invaded the area in the left chest housing a twig of the vagus nerve called the left recurrent laryngeal nerve. It energizes the vocal cord so it can move during speech. That nerve twig was heavily invaded by the cancer and had to be removed. Now the left vocal cord, without its nerve, would need to be surgically moved over to share vibration with the right one for speaking. This procedure was considered minor, though, and would be done easily as an outpatient in Austin.

Thus, Mark was sent post-op to ICU minus his left lung, his left pulmonary artery, and his left recurrent laryngeal nerve, but plus a big Dacron graft in his aorta. His team of doctors watched him recuperate first there, then several days later in a stepdown or lesser care unit. Thankfully, he again followed his routine post-op course of doing well, recovering quickly, and then coming home, despite some frightening moments when it seemed there might be an air leak from the resected lung. A bronchoscopy, or endoscope looking down the trachea or windpipe, showed that all was intact, however. Mark recuperated quickly and was discharged less than a week later to his and Nancy's hotel where, according to Mark, "We just hung out."

The pathology report, normally a one-liner or so in most surgeries, ran four pages, confirming that this tumor was indeed a recurrence of his original testicular cancer in 1999. Officially it was termed. "...a late relapse of a nonseminomatous germ cell cancer of testicular origin extensively involving the aorticopulmonary window." Cancer had returned with a vengeance to a very vulnerable place in Mark's body.

The good news was that all twenty of the removed lymph nodes had not been invaded by the cancer. The other good news was that Dr. Kesler had successfully excised the entirety of the tumor.

That Mark recovered so quickly and so well from such an invasive surgery was a testimony both to the outstanding surgical skills of Dr. Kesler and his team, as well as to Mark's determination to return quickly to his normal state. As Mark had been told after the 2010 surgery, he could have no more chemo; his blood vessels would be unable to handle it.

Mark's job now was to recuperate slowly. This surgery had been invasive, and two major organs had been compromised; the trauma to his body this time was significant. He could not expect the usual paradigm of surgery/recuperate/return to work after so great a bodily insult. Dr. Kesler also stressed that if Mark had any oral procedure, even a dental cleaning, he would need antibiotics in advance.

There were some tender moments after surgery. Dr. Einhorn personally delivered joyful news during a hospital visit with Nancy and Mark, "Your AFP is now normal. Congratulations, you can now go home and raise your children."

What a milestone! They had never heard those words after previous surgeries. Mark, of course, asked what the AFP value was; pre-op, it had been over 200. When Dr. Einhorn told him it was six, he replied, always competitive, "Four is better."

In his usual to-the-point manner, cardiothoracic surgeon Dr. Kesler said to Mark, "Now you can say without a doubt that you are cancer-free."

Despite all the pain, the inconvenience, fear, and doubt…, all of us felt at that moment enormous gratitude for Mark's medical team and for Mark's own bravery and aplomb in the face of this massive surgery. As in the past, before leaving the hospital, Nancy and Mark made the rounds to the staff, thanking them for their part in helping him heal.

Back in Austin, Nancy made follow-up appointments to check on Mark's progress. She found a cardiothoracic surgeon in town to assess him. An X-ray and an exam were done, and all was well. It was now nearly August, and the kids were getting ready to return to school. Even though he understood all the implications of such a huge surgery, he was anxious to get back to normal and back to work; he just wasn't there yet, but he felt he should be. At each doctor visit, however, including one back in Indiana in August, Mark and Nancy were told, "You've just had major life-threatening surgery, lost a lung, have a graft in your aorta, got cleared of cancer, and are older than when you had surgeries in 1999, 2001, and 2010. You have to have patience. Certainly you are tired; who wouldn't be? Now you just need to rest, eat right and gradually add some exercise."

This all made perfect sense; yet Mark somehow sensed that this time, things were different, ominous, and unfamiliar. He couldn't explain why he had these feelings, but they tormented him.

Mark was a seasoned cancer survivor. He knew well how his body handled recovery from surgery. His lack of stamina nagged at him: just helping Nancy clean his beloved hot tub, normally a minor task, put him to bed for an entire day. He complained of shortness of breath, but hadn't he just lost a lung? A doctor's visit confirmed, however, that his oxygen levels were normal at 99% saturation, even with only one lung. What was the problem, then? He told himself to be patient. But the feelings of uneasiness were never far from his mind.

After about six weeks, the time had come to have his paralyzed left vocal cord medialized, or moved over to touch the right one, allowing both vocal cords to vibrate when he spoke. This would require only a simple day surgery in Austin. Merely the thought of being in a hospital environment again caused Mark anguish; still, though, he proceeded.

Mark came through that day surgery without a problem; however, he started to hiccup repeatedly a few days later. Follow-up visits to the ear/ nose/ throat doctor noted this phenomenon was not uncommon with vocal cord surgery. Mark's side-effect was abnormal, however, because he continued hiccupping for twenty-four hours straight, getting no sleep and using energy that he could ill-afford to waste. He was prescribed several medications, but each had poor success and intolerable side effects.

Mark also continued to feel short of breath, which worried him incessantly. His left chest also hurt, but he had just undergone a brutal and invasive left chest surgery. Was he, only six weeks out from major surgery, making too much of this discomfort?

Mark continued to struggle with what was happening. Just recuperating seemed to wear him out, but it always came back to the same reason: he was recovering from major surgery. He was now forty years old. This all made sense to everyone, including Mark. But he felt tired *all* the time. He told Nancy he felt a "vacuum feeling" in his chest when he ate, but he was unable to describe it well. Mark just was not himself. He had now been out of work since July, two whole months; this was unheard of for him. He wanted to get back to work; he wanted his "normal" back.

And it was, in a way. The kids were back in school. Late in August, the four Cliftons attended a friend's fortieth birthday party; pictures taken there show Mark looking well, smiling into the camera as he shared a couch with two of his best buddies. Tabor and Marshall dressed up in funny glasses and wigs for a photoshoot. Everyone had a great time. This, Mark thought, was almost normal.

On Friday, September 13, Nancy drove Tabor to an overnight stay at the Waco Zoo with a school group. She called me from there, asking that I check on Mark by phone. I did; he seemed exhausted and did hiccup. I could tell he was frustrated but he didn't seem to be in dire straits. I was a bit concerned but not overly so; after all, I reasoned like everyone else, he had just had yet another surgery shortly after a brutal one just six weeks ago. He had been examined by several doctors. His vital signs, oxygen saturation, and chest X-ray were all normal. Insecure, however, I called one of my fellow ear/nose/throat specialists in Dallas who agreed with the therapy Mark was receiving. Everyone agreed that "this too shall pass."

When Nancy and Tabor got home the next day, Mark still was not feeling well. The hiccups had worn him out. Even though he'd been told that hiccups were associated with the neck surgery, Mark felt blindsided by how much it exhausted him. Nancy decided that, come Monday, she was going to take him back to the doctor. Little did she know that Monday, September 16, 2013, would involve far more than a doctor visit; it would become a date forever etched in her mind.

CHAPTER 17

• • •

September 16, 2013

Around four o'clock in the morning, Mark woke Nancy and told her he felt terrible. He was having some diarrhea, maybe a bit of fever. Nancy called me right away. This was our normal SOP: she and I had over the years often joked about how handy it was to have free medical advice from the family doctor who had been involved in Mark's medical case since Day One. After some discussion, I agreed with her decision to get him in to see his Austin primary care doctor later that morning.

About an hour later, Nancy called again. This was not normal. Mark was now vomiting along with the diarrhea, and now there was blood in both. He was so weak he could hardly get back to bed from the bathroom. Since the kids would be getting up for school in just a few hours, Nancy wanted to call Wade to take Mark to the ER, but Mark refused, insisting he was afraid he would "mess up" his dad's car. I told her, "Get off the phone now, call 911, and keep me in the loop. If you need me, call me."

By 7:00 a.m., I was my office; Nancy had not called, so I just dismissed this as yet another scare. Mark had been through some tough medical times in the past. He was a warrior and had always done well; after all, he had just had the big July surgery and then the vocal cord surgery less than a week before. The hiccups had worn him out. I figured there would be a clear reason after the ER workup and that soon he would be fine.

But still, fever and bloody vomiting and diarrhea: those symptoms gnawed at me; I wondered if he had picked up a virus somewhere. I reminded myself that he was in the ER and would be diagnosed soon, if not already. Around 11:00, my office was in full swing. Suddenly, my office manager, Monica, interrupted me with a tap on the exam room door. "Nancy's on the phone."

I took the call in my office; Nancy's voice was shaky and tearful.

"It's really bad this time, Mom. We had an argument last night, and I think I hurt Mark's heart. They're taking him to the heart lab."

CHAPTER 18

• • •

THE HEART LAB. *THAT'S THE Cardiac Cath Lab*, I thought. This must have something to do with that graft in his aorta. But as I mentally ran through a differential diagnosis, I just couldn't see any probable connection between his aorta, and the vomiting, diarrhea and fever. I assured her that their argument had had nothing to do with whatever was happening with his heart. But I was at a loss to explain what the problem was.

"Do you want me to come now?"

"Yes," she said in a whisper, her voice quivering. "I'm just so scared."

I had been in private medical family practice over twenty-three years, and I had never walked out of my office full of patients. They had always been my first priority, as I had agreed to when I took the Hippocratic Oath in 1986. But never had I felt Nancy's fear like this. I left.

I had Monica cancel the rest of the office day and drove the 185 miles as fast as I dared to St. David's Hospital in Round Rock. Still in my scrubs, around 1:00, I walked into the ICU waiting room where a crowd of family and friends had already formed. I held Nancy as she cried. The Cardiac Cath Lab surgeon had not yet come from downstairs to talk to Nancy, so none of us knew any details; all we knew was that this was serious.

CHAPTER 19

• • •

WHEN I HAD TOLD NANCY to call 911, that's exactly what she did. Then she called Wade. She'd needed him to stay at Mark's side in the hospital for a few hours so she could get the kids ready for school. Mark had disagreed with involving his father, and he and Nancy had argued. The paramedics and Wade arrived at almost the same time.

The paramedics were as quiet as possible, respecting Nancy's request that the kids not witness whatever they needed to do with Mark. She stood outside of Tabor's bedroom and Wade stood guard before Marshall's, in case the kids woke up and were frightened.

The EMTs realized that they needed to transport Mark, and in a hurry. His blood pressure was dangerously low, his heart rate dangerously high. But their gurney would not make the sharp turn needed to get Mark down the stairs.

They improvised, using a heavy wooden kitchen chair. Although she did not admit it at the time, Tabor woke up and figured out what was going on, but lay frozen in bed. Marshall, the champion sleeper in the family, mercifully slept through it all.

As the EMTs were carrying Mark out the front door, he told them to stop. He had something he felt compelled to say to Nancy. Impatient, Nancy shot him a questioning look. He looked up at her and used words from one of their favorite songs, "I want to grow old with you."

Nancy's face melted with emotion. She knew then how scared Mark really was.

Mark was taken by ambulance to Saint David's ER in Round Rock that morning, but nobody there knew anything about him. He had never been to that hospital before. His recent vocal cord surgery was in a nearby Austin facility, and his chest surgeries had both been in Indiana. Wade was the first of the family to arrive, since Nancy had taken the kids to school. She would join him as soon as she could. Wade described the scenario:

> "It was 5:00 in the morning and dark outside. I didn't know the area and had to make a couple of passes to find the place. They let me into his room, and when I got in there, it was in panic mode; ER staff were everywhere; it was truly an emergency situation. I was only able to just hold his hand and stay out of their way. He had almost no blood pressure. All they wanted to do was to get blood into him as fast as they could. Nobody said anything to me. They were focused exclusively on Mark."

Mark's chief complaint was bloody stool, bloody vomit and fever; the source of the problem was initially suspected to be bleeding in the gastrointestinal (GI) tract. When asked in the ambulance if he had been taking anti-inflammatories, Mark admitted that he had, since he was weaning off the narcotics he had been given from both of his recent surgeries. That could explain the bleeding. But what caused the fever? Further, why would he have an infection in the GI tract, and if so, where would it be? It was clear from the beginning that Mark's diagnosis would not be simple to make.

His initial lab values caused even more concern for the ER doctor; Mark had a very low hematocrit and a high platelet count, together indicating that he was bleeding a lot and had been for a long time. Dr. John Ziebert, a gastroenterologist, came at once and planned an upper endoscopy on the spot. This literal "inside look" involves anesthetizing the back of the throat to inhibit the gag reflex. A tube with a built-in camera and biopsy forceps is then fed into the patient's mouth, down the esophagus and into the stomach for a real-time view of what is bleeding and how much.

Nancy arrived at that point. When told that an endoscopy was planned, she demanded to speak to Dr. Ziebert to be sure he knew all of Mark's recent serious history. As she filled him in, Dr. Ziebert's eyes widened; all he knew at that point was that a young man was bleeding seriously from his gastrointestinal tract and that he had been on anti-inflammatories. He called Mark's primary care office, who faxed the full history; he still had to do the procedure, of course, but he proceeded with even further caution, unsure exactly what all he would find in Mark's esophagus. In less than a few minutes, he found out.

What he saw was revealing and terrifying at the same time. Mark was, indeed, bleeding, but not from the stomach, although the scope could see, according to Dr. Ziebert's operative report "…a whole lot of blood down in the stomach…" He then noted the true source of Mark's problem, "…an adherent, thumb-sized clot over a pulsatile esophageal ulceration."

An ulceration meant there was a hole in the esophagus: dangerous, but not yet deadly, since the bleeding had already clotted. The clot was adherent, fixed in place. A thumb-sized clot was quite large, since the esophageal diameter is only about half an inch. By far, however, the most ominous finding was that a pulse was seen under that clot. This meant that a nearby large artery was also involved. If this was the aorta pulsating, maybe it too was bleeding. And if the clot broke off, especially if the blood forming it was coming mostly from the aorta, it would cause an avalanche of blood and instant death.

Dr. Zeibert knew that the fragile clot was the only thing keeping Mark from bleeding to death. Dislodging it would have been the equivalent of removing a finger from a hole in a leaking bucket. He gingerly tiptoed his scope around it. As his report read, "…the scope was able to be passed beyond this without disrupting the clot….at the termination of the procedure the clot was adherent to the esophageal wall." That was the good news: the blood clot was stable. In the impression section of his operative report, though, he listed "probable aortoesophageal fistula."

Bad news. A fistula is a fragile bridge that forms between two hollow conduits in the body, most often between two blood vessels, but in Mark's case, between the aorta and the esophagus.

The concept is like the pipes in your front yard. There, the two main hollow conduits are: one carrying clean water from the street to the house, and the other carrying waste-contaminated water from the house to the street. Assume those two pipes lie side by side, and there's a break in the waste water conduit that rots and eats into the fresh water conduit. Once a break occurs, an area of high turbulence results since the pipe's inside surface is no longer smooth. Anything in the flow of waste will catch and build up, exactly at that spot. Thus, sewage buildup there will allow the fistula or bridge to form, enlarge, then rot, and over time, become a filthy connection between the two conduits. The result: contamination from the dirty water into the clean, and waste of the clean water into the dirty. In Mark's case, Dr. Ziebert suspected a mixing of pure sterile aortic blood with contaminated esophageal contents such as food, air, and saliva. That situation is life-threatening.

To confirm his suspicions, Dr. Ziebert ordered a CT/angiogram (CTA). This test, which shows blood flow in arteries, confirmed that, yes, the aorta was bleeding, and yes, there was this abnormal connection between the esophagus and the aorta. But that was not all: the aorta was also bleeding into the chest cavity lining called the pleura. The report noted, "…what appears to be …an aortic/enteric fistula and an aortic pleural fistula."

Translated, this means there were two fistulas, two rickety bridges of tissue. The aortic/enteric fistula had formed between Mark's aorta and his esophagus. Anything from the esophagus going anywhere except to the stomach would be a huge source of infection. In Mark's case, his oral intake and usual mouth bacteria were being carried not just into his stomach as they should, but also were being dumped directly through the fragile fistula, into the pristine aorta.

The second fistula was stuck between the aorta and the lining of the empty lung cavity. There, in Mark's empty chest cavity, the aorta leaked fresh blood, and the esophagus leaked bacteria-laden oral contents, forming an enlarging lake of contagion.

That slimy mess then connected not just to the esophagus and pleural lining; it adhered to Mark's aortic Dacron graft. This cloth graft or patch was basically sopping up the contaminated esophageal contents mixed with blood, adding to the spread of infection. It was a perfect storm of pathological events: a dirty and leaking esophagus, seeping its contents into the aorta; a slowly-growing pool of bloody pus and air in the pleural lining; and, most importantly, an aorta leaking blood, even further compromised by an infected Dacron graft.

How much blood was involved? The average adult male has about ten units (roughly pints) of whole blood, comprised mainly of plasma and packed red blood cells. Platelets are there too, but are tiny in size with lots of surface area and taking up very little space. The total blood fluid is around 4.7 liters, over a gallon.

Mark's normal hemoglobin ran between 15-16 grams; when he had reached the ER that morning, his hemoglobin had been 7.0; he had already lost roughly half of his blood. He was transfused quickly with four units of packed red blood cells in the ER, but he was still bleeding, mainly from the aorta. Blood was also seeping into the esophagus and running down into the stomach, as well as into the pleural lining of his left chest.

The aorta is the largest and strongest artery in the body, over an inch in diameter. It acts as a superhighway carrying sterile freshly-oxygenated blood straight from the left heart. That blood, coursing through the aorta, is the cleanest it will ever be. Any infectious contamination in the aorta from any source can permeate all the systems of the adult body in about a minute, the human circulatory rate while at rest. Thus, contamination from the aortoesophageal fistula had been coursing throughout Mark's entire body for an unknown but significant length of time.

Dr. Ziebert immediately told Nancy his findings of the upper endoscopy and CTA, both of which had already implicated the aorta and its infected graft as the major players in this drama. An ECHO, also known as a heart sonogram, showed that Mark's heart function had already declined, with an ejection fraction (EF), or the amount of blood pushed out of the heart with each heartbeat, of 62.2%. A normal EF is 64%-83%; thus, Mark's was not yet emergent. However, if that clot seen in the endoscopy were suddenly to break off, the EF would plummet, and Mark would bleed to death quickly. Dr. Ziebert told Nancy that he had little hope that Mark could survive all this; he then put into motion a call for a cardiothoracic surgeon.

That cardiothoracic surgeon, Dr. Reginald Baptiste, was in a meeting in downtown Austin, interviewing faculty candidates for the future UT Austin Dell Medical School. He at first deflected the call, but when he was told that a St. David's administrator was on the line and needed him STAT at St. David's in Round Rock, Dr. Baptiste knew something serious was happening. He answered. Then he left.

After examining Mark and reviewing his case, Dr. Baptiste approached Nancy and other family members who had by then arrived at the hospital. He reviewed the grim findings briefly: first, the upper endoscopy, identifying the clot, and suggesting a fistula with contamination between the aorta and the esophagus, thus spreading bacterial infection with every heartbeat; second, the CTA also showing IV contrast dripping out of the aorta and into both the left pleural lining and into the esophagus, thus confirming a life-threatening aortic bleed; and finally, the ECHO, showing an early but not-yet life-threatening decrease of heart functioning.

If that dripping hole in the aorta were not repaired immediately, Mark could easily die within minutes from bleeding, or within hours to days from sepsis, or massive infection.

Nancy and the family listened while Dr. Baptiste laid out his plan. Mark's biggest threat was obviously from bleeding. He had already lost a lot of blood; although he had quickly been transfused with those four units of PRBC's, he already needed more. The plan was to patch the graft and aorta at this point, just to get the bleeding to stop. The esophagus would have to wait; the goal at this point was for the aorta to once again become a leak-free, one-way conduit exclusively for clean blood out of the left ventricle, just as it had been originally designed.

To save time and to be the least invasive while still getting the job done, Dr. Baptiste planned to do this from the inside out: go up the groin, inside the aorta, and put patching "balloons" wherever the aorta or graft was leaking. It was a gamble with no alternatives. Mark could easily bleed to death despite being already transfused aggressively; he could die of widespread infection from the esophagus leaking into the aorta; or, even worse, if the graft fell apart at any time, he would die instantly. These life-threatening issues were simultaneous, but first and foremost, the bleeding had to be stopped. Now. Nancy understood and signed the consent form. With the aid of the workup so far and with the clock ticking, Dr. Baptiste and his team rolled Mark quickly into the Cardiac Cath Lab.

It was a group effort for sure, but Dr. Baptiste was unquestionably the captain of the ship. The ultimate idea was not to repair or remove the aortic graft, but to put a number of smaller stents inside of it, thus accomplishing two things: to squeeze off the bleeding by putting balloons inside the leaking aortic wall and to block off the area where the esophageal contents were contaminating the aortic blood flow.

This sounds like a straightforward solution: like slipping some smaller caliber clean pipes inside of a leaking larger dirty one, but it was anything but simple or easy. In fact, it took a total of seven different balloon stents inside of Mark's aorta: four higher up, two in the middle and one in the lower part of the old graft. Each stent had to be perfectly placed, despite Mark's bleeding throughout the entire procedure.

During this complex procedure, the Cath Lab was a world of tension with multiple doctors, nurses, and technicians doing all they could to beat the clock as Mark's life slipped away. It required exquisite finesse from all involved. Every second counted. The glass-walled control room overlooking the lab was also packed with hospital personnel both directly and indirectly involved in Mark's care. Even the hospital CEO attended. Nancy, family members, and her pastor remained in the Cath waiting room, praying and sobbing.

The thought was ever present that this forty-year-old could die right before their eyes. And, in medical-speak, he did, twice. After the stents were placed, Mark's heart "coded" into a lethal rhythm, requiring powerful drugs, electrical shocks and CPR. The treatment protocol is brutal and seldom effective, especially in a very ill patient like Mark.

Dr. Baptiste, despite all his expertise and intervention, realized Mark was not going to survive. He came out of the Cath Lab and slowly squatted down in front of Nancy, who by that time was slumped on a couch in the waiting room.

"I'm sorry," he told her, looking directly into her eyes. "We did everything we could, but he's not going to make it. I'm going to go back in, get him cleaned up, and then you can come in and say your goodbyes." Then he returned to the Cath Lab.

Nancy was already crying, but these words destroyed her, and she sank to the floor. Mark's family members were in shock too. Nancy's first thought was of Tabor and Marshall. "What am I going to say to the kids?" she sobbed. Everyone in the room clung to one another, weeping. There were no answers.

Suddenly, the Cath Lab doors swung open and Mark was being rolled out on a gurney. What? Didn't Dr. Baptiste just say that Mark was going to die? Weren't they supposed to go in and say goodbye? Dr. Baptiste paused in front of Nancy.

"We've got a heartbeat. I don't know if he'll even make it upstairs, but we're going to try."

With that, Mark's gurney, Dr. Baptiste, and support staff slipped into the elevator, on the way to ICU.

By that time, Mark had received ten more units of packed red blood cells, plus fourteen units of fresh frozen plasma. He was still alive, but barely. The good news was that a post-procedure thoracic arteriogram (arterial contrast pictures taken after the seven stents were put in) showed that the stenting procedure was a success. The operative report read, "…excellent flow throughout the thoracic aorta with exclusion of the previous extravasation and no evidence of active arterial extravasation at this time." Aortic blood was going where it was supposed to go and not going where it wasn't. Despite this morsel of good news, Dr. Baptiste ended his report with, "Condition: grave." Recovery was not expected.

Nancy met Dr. Baptiste upstairs in the ICU waiting area just outside the staff elevator. Mark was lying unmoving on a gurney, on life support, his eyes taped shut. Nancy was allowed one kiss, and then he was swept into ICU.

Dr. Baptiste told Nancy that the battle for Mark's life was not over. He and his team would soon need to return to that left chest cavity to look at the damage to the esophagus, clean out whatever contagion was there, and inspect the graft from inside the chest wall. That would have to wait a day or two until Mark could be stabilized, if indeed he could be stabilized. Dr. Baptiste emphasized, "This is incredibly risky for an already traumatized and stressed body."

As successful as Dr. Baptiste's medical skills were, Mark was still in bad shape. His kidneys were suffering from low blood pressure stemming both from blood loss and the massive infection itself, commonly called septic shock. When Mark left the Cath Lab, he was on three different drugs (pressors) to prevent his blood pressure from collapsing.

Mark's blood sugars soared and had to be controlled with an insulin drip. Emergency medications to normalize elevated potassium, creatinine, and calcium levels were put into place. Other measures to increase his dangerously low pH and oxygen levels, were used. Throughout all of this, Mark was given several potent broad spectrum antibiotics to cover the infection.

At some time in the distant future, the infected graft, even with the seven new stents in the repaired aorta, would need to be replaced. It was made of Dacron and thus had no blood supply. This meant there was no way for antibiotics, carried in the bloodstream, to reach the site of infection.

Aware of the gravity of the situation, Mark's nurses juggled with medications and equipment all through that first night, just to keep him alive. Dr. Baptiste had made it clear to them too: this critically ill man was going to have to go to the OR in twenty-four to forty-eight hours to clean out the cesspool that remained inside him. Now that the bleeding had been stopped, the top priority became clearing the contagion in his chest; no cocktail of antibiotics alone could clear that up. Antibiotics were, so to speak, killing the alligators in the swamp; Dr. Baptiste and his surgical team would have to go in surgically and drain it. Thus, directed by Dr. Baptiste, the ICU nurses worked unceasingly during the night of September 16 to keep Mark alive.

September 17 dawned; Mark was still alive! Room 5 in ICU was a flurry of activity, with multiple specialists, each caring for a separate organ system: heart, lungs, kidneys, brain, and infection of all the above, just to name a few. No laboratory values were optimal, but at least none was incompatible with life. On his rounds, Dr. Baptiste again and again stressed the gravity of Mark's situation.

On September 18, Dr. Baptiste once more told Nancy that he was surprised Mark was still with us, that a normal healthy person could certainly not have survived the many traumas Mark had faced and was still facing. And, despite all the imaging, he had no real way of knowing what he would find in Mark's chest, but he knew it was not going to be good. He had discussed his findings and treatment so far with Dr. Kesler in Indiana, who, although saddened with the bad news, agreed with Dr. Baptiste's plan of care. Dr. Baptiste stressed to Nancy that Mark's "… health challenges are going to be critical, complicated, and long-term." He informed her that if she chose to do nothing, that was acceptable too; Mark's chances of survival were almost negligible.

My older daughter, Carol, had flown in from Boston. Mark was never alone; family members took around-the-clock shifts in ICU Room 5. He remained unresponsive. Nancy kept their children at home; at first, they didn't want to go to school, but after they spent a day with church friends, she felt they needed a sense of normalcy. Davis Elementary allowed

Tabor and Marshall to go to the counselor's office at any time they felt overwhelmed. They both found themselves there often. As Tabor put it, "I want everyone to stop looking at me."

CHAPTER 20

• • •

Two days after Mark's crisis, with heavy hearts, Mark's and my families met in the ICU hallway to help Nancy with the decision: proceed with surgery, or let Mark go. We all held hands, crying, praying. After much pro and con from everyone present, each person had a final say, and then Nancy had to make *the* decision. It was an awful moment for her.

"If he dies on the table, I won't be there with him, and I want to be. But if I don't try, I'll never know. I know he would want me to go for it, just like always. I'm just not ready to say goodbye."

Thus, surgery was a go, starting at 8:30 a.m. Nancy kissed him good-bye, not sure she'd ever see him alive again. He, of course, did not respond; nobody knew if he ever could again.

During the previous three days, an endless procession of family and friends had filed through the ICU waiting room. At one time, over thirty of us stood by. I spoke with the CEO of St. David's, hoping that in our grief we weren't interfering with other patients' families and their own problems. There were platters of food, towers of soft drinks, plenty of snacks and dips from well-wishers in the crowded ICU waiting room. The CEO was kind and understanding with all the tears, fears, and confusion we were experiencing, assuring us that St. David's was there for us.

There were so many of Mark's bosses and coworkers there that morning, men and women who were smart, tough, movers and shakers at Dell in Austin. Yet, to a person, their faces were grief-stricken and their eyes, red and swollen from crying. Some sobbed openly.

Prayer groups came too, neighbors, parents of Tabor's and Marshall's classmates, their family pastor, friends both from Austin and from several hundred miles away. Some Mark had not seen since high school.

Those hours in the OR passed slowly as Dr. Baptiste's team worked on Mark. Mostly we all prayed and kept quiet conversations going to pass the time. It went on and on. This time for Nancy it was totally different, though. In the past, Mark's cancer surgeries had always been on a basically healthy young man. At forty, he was still young, but now his body was barely surviving.

Minutes dragged to hours. We had run out of banal conversation. It's hard to make small talk when someone you love is just down the hall, fighting for his life. There were some periods of silence in the waiting room, punctuated by an occasional half-hearted laugh. Finally, at 12:44 p.m. Dr. Baptiste called us to the designated family room in ICU. His smile was a signal that Mark had survived; he told us he was going to finish his paperwork, then meet with us to discuss details.

While we waited in that tiny room we started with a prayer from each as we held hands awaiting the details. Wade's prayer said it all. "Lord, just hold him in your arms." Tears streamed from all of us. We ran out of tissues and had to find more. Then talk wandered to Mark's family reminiscences; Kellye said, "Remember the time we saw that huge snake at the ranch, and we all ran?"

Smiles, some quiet laughter—anything to fill the time until we knew what Mark would be facing. It was an eternity of waiting but with one difference from just three days ago: we knew at least that Mark was still alive.

Dr. Baptiste finally arrived with one of his surgical residents in tow. He stood just inside the door since the family filled the room. *A perfect get-away position if he needs it*, I thought, my mind wandering. I also figured that as he had just dictated his operative report, he had probably, at least subconsciously, rehearsed how to tell this frightened family all the bad news of what had to be inside Mark's chest. Now, in front of us, he spoke softly but confidently. He often gestured and I noticed his hands:

perfect, strong, long-fingered surgeon's hands. My surgical colleagues had hands like his; I felt Mark was literally in good hands.

He told us that Mark was stable but in bad shape. The very good news was that there had been no more bleeding. The seven stents had done their job, both preventing further blood loss and not allowing further contamination into the bloodstream. The bad news was that the infection was even greater than had originally been thought. He told us that he and his team found cesspools of infection nearly everywhere, particularly down in the left chest close to the stomach and up near the graft in the aorta. As best they could, they had cut away and cleansed as much dead tissue and filth as possible, then rinsed the cavity with liter after liter of warm sterile saline or saltwater. This is called debridement and irrigation.

To cleanse continuously, a double chest tube was placed high up in the top of Mark's left chest cavity. Through the tubes ran multiple high-powered antibiotics to cover the contamination that had certainly come from the esophagus. Cultures of the purulence were sent for identification to fine-tune care later. At the lower back of Mark's chest was an exit chest tube, hooked up to continuous suction, thus directing the antibiotic cocktail in at the top and suctioning it out through the bottom of the infected chest cavity. This created a sort of push/pull dynamic to continue scrubbing out the fetid mess.

Dr. Baptiste then told us what was the most difficult for us to hear and for him to relay. Opening Marks's left chest cavity, he had trouble figuring out just what was in there; it was a rotten surgical field. One of his assistants would later tell us with tears in her eyes that it had smelled like stool. Familiar landmarks such as the far end of the esophagus could not even be identified in the foul-smelling mess. Dr. Baptiste showed us a cell-phone picture a nurse had taken; it was just a brown slimy smear. Even as a doctor, I couldn't identify one familiar structure.

As they debrided and irrigated, they were amazed that they were unable to find much of Mark's distal or lower esophagus down near his stomach; it seemed like it had just rotted away, like a washed-out bridge. Reeling from this information, we formulated questions one by one.

How long had that huge mess been in there? How had Mark managed to continue to get around for so long? No wonder he complained of not feeling as well as he thought he should. Was this that "vacuum feeling" he had complained about but had never been able to describe fully? Dr. Baptiste's answer to all these questions was simply, "I don't know; he has to be the strongest, most patient, most pain-tolerant man on earth." Dr. Baptiste then explained further that he and his team had fished around near Mark's neck and found that the upper or proximal esophagus was actually intact and healthy. They tunneled this upper stump under the soft tissues of his left neck, bending and redirecting it; his esophagus, what was left of it, would now empty its contents out of a stoma or hole above his left collarbone. A small ostomy bag was now attached there. The whole concept is commonly called a "spit valve" since saliva is produced continuously and needs a bag to collect it when it can't be swallowed.

Dr. Baptiste added that he had spoken to Dr. Kesler, Mark's Indiana cardiothoracic surgeon. Both of them had agreed the spit valve procedure was necessary. He stopped, giving us time to wrap our heads around this bizarre medical information. None of us had ever heard of a rotten esophagus or a spit valve; even as a long-time physician, I certainly never had.

Nancy, of course, was the first to process this information.

"I can tell you for sure that when my husband wakes up with a bag on his neck, he's going to be pissed!"

My outspoken daughter; this sounded just like her. I wondered how a highly skilled cardiothoracic surgeon who had literally saved Mark's life a few days ago, who had bent over backwards rushing to St. David's as soon as he could, who had meticulously but swiftly and correctly triaged Mark's problems, addressed and successfully treated them one by one—how was this amazing gentleman, standing in front of the whole family, in this time of raw nerves and grief, going to respond? I held my breath.

Dr. Baptiste just smiled wryly, gestured with those beautiful hands and quietly answered, "Ya think?"

It was perfect: the tension evaporated, we all laughed, and I know everyone was thinking: *We hope and pray with all our hearts that Mark sticks around to be pissed.*

Serious again, Nancy persisted, "So how can he stay alive, if everything he eats comes out in a bag?"

Ah, a perfect segue; Dr. Baptiste first assured us that TPN or total parental nutrition, feeding through a vein, had already begun. He then explained that he had implanted a feeding tube into an incision in Mark's abdomen. This, of course, was no simple gastric tube or G-tube that many of us are familiar with. This was a GJ-tube.

Even though there would be only one tube sticking out of Mark's abdomen, that tube had two separate ports, one dumping directly into the stomach, and the other dumping further along into the small intestine or jejunum. Because Mark was so severely infected, the J-tube port would be used first, bypassing and resting the stomach and instead dumping directly into the jejunum. Later, the simpler, larger, and more direct G-tube port would be opened, directly into the stomach. Although Dr. Baptiste did not elaborate on it then, the GJ-tube would later become a major annoyance, because even the most seasoned medical staff members were unfamiliar with it.

That was a lot of information to process. The implications of time frame could not even be hinted at. An ostomy on a neck? An ostomy is usually on the abdomen, hidden and considered an embarrassing nuisance. How long would that have to go on? And if the feeding tube implanted in the abdominal wall had two ports for two different time frames, when would all that be over? The future seemed to be slipping further and further distant, like a beach ball on the ocean. As my thoughts wandered in that direction, Dr. Baptiste drew us back quickly to an even more significant issue.

"But back to the aorta; remember that the repairs to it are only temporary. That graft's going to have to be replaced. I've got a specialist in Houston who can do that surgery after all the infection is cleared and Mark is doing well."

But that will be months down the road, I thought.

My daughter Carol whispered to me, "...if Mark makes it that far."

Dr. Baptiste then briefly told us a bit more about the esophageal ostomy or spit valve, noting that it too would be temporary. It could be removed and the lower esophagus remade at the same time and in the same operating room in Houston when the aortic graft would be replaced. A second cardiothoracic surgeon, who would oversee removing the spit valve, was more specialized in dealing with the esophagus. Dr. Baptiste knew both Houston cardiothoracic surgeons, and both doctors were well-known, respected in their fields, and comfortable working together.

We were winding down; the most pressing issues had been answered. Dr. Baptiste asked if there was anything else. Kim, Mark's sister spoke up.

"What about his right lung? Is it up to the job?"

Dr. Baptiste smiled. Here was a ray of good news; the right lung was doing just fine, carrying both its load and a lot of the absent left lung's, too.

"And his heart?" Nancy asked. "How strong is it now?"

Another smile from Dr. Baptiste. "His heart is in great shape." He summed up by telling us how gravely ill Mark still was, but stressed that Mark had to have been somehow constitutionally and psychologically beyond exceptional to have withstood and survived all that he had endured over the last few days. He expressed admiration for Mark, saying how he had to be a fighter to have kept going, most likely for weeks, while the infection was raging in his body. He left us with the thought that, while Mark was now in critical condition, the situation was not hopeless, based on all he had seen and treated so far. The best thing Mark could get from us as a family was our presence, our love, our voices, and our encouragement.

In that small room, we were all overwhelmed, both with gratitude that Mark had survived so far and with all the work that remained to be done in the future.

Over the next day or two, we were to meet the myriad of specialists on Mark's case. They made a constant parade in and out of ICU Room 5. Dr. Baptiste and his cardiothoracic surgery team were in the lead, of course. Mark's neurologist was testing to see if any "dirty bombs" had ridden along the carotid arteries from the contaminated aorta, ending up in the brain. His pulmonologist saw to the ventilator, reviewing his chest X-rays; his ID or infectious disease specialist ran cultures to identify which bacteria were making him so sick and adjusting his antibiotics accordingly; his renal specialist kept an eye on decreased kidney function and abnormal blood sugars, and of course, his ICU intensivist, the coordinator of the entire team, made sure nothing slipped through the cracks. We all sat poised to see when Mark would wake up.

Despite this truly intensive care, though, Mark remained unresponsive, even to noxious stimuli, like squeezing his toe or touching the white of his eye with a cotton swab. All who visited were profoundly saddened by Mark's inert body lying in the bed, a ventilator breathing for him, and surrounded by ominous beeping machines, confusing arrays of IV drips, and huge monitors with all kinds of incomprehensible zigzagging information. In these faces, I saw disbelief, fear and awe at this vigorous young man they had known, now reduced to an inert stranger lying immobile on the sheets.

Each day was much like the one before. There had been concern about a possible stroke due to massive blood loss and subsequent low blood pressure. Mark did move his head and shoulders once to voice, and we all rejoiced, but we weren't sure what that signified. His right great toe began to lose its pink color and became quite blue and cold, probably caused by a tiny "dirty bomb" septic embolus showered from the aorta after the fistula formed. If a dirty embolus had made it to his toe, could one have made it to his brain as well? His neurologist ordered an MRI to see.

Sure enough, there were six septic emboli or tiny strokes in the brain. His neurologist went over the films with both of my daughters and me; she noted they were very small and most likely would affect Mark little, if at all. Mark's brain blood vessels were in good shape overall and could handle this onslaught of tiny pieces of infection. She smiled her encouragement to us and told us not to waste our worry on this. Here was at least some good news in all the bad news we'd been coping with.

And there was plenty of bad news. From the massive sepsis and related issues, Mark's lab numbers showed failure of kidneys and liver, as well as anemia and malnutrition. His pancreas couldn't keep up with the demands for insulin production so his blood sugar went out of control. In a few days, his temperature spiked to 104 degrees. His blood cultures grew out five different bacteria and one strain of yeast, most assuredly from his esophagus. A brain CT scan showed swelling, thought to be due to infection. His body swelled too. The words "severe debility" appeared on his chart. There was talk of dialysis to relieve his kidneys from damage caused by decreased blood flow. Amputation of that blue great toe was considered. Good news seemed nowhere to be found. Every day, we were told that it was a miracle that he was still alive.

Distraught about Mark's unresponsiveness, Nancy asked me to start inquiries into planning Mark's funeral so she could stay at the hospital. I had met Merrill, Mark's and Nancy's pastor, so I leaned heavily on him to walk me through that most horrendous task. Talking about cremation, church services, and funeral homes was repulsive, surreal. Carol, my older daughter, and I shopped for black dress clothes. She would tell me later, "I have never cried so hard, so long, or so often in my life as I did while I was in Texas." How could it be that we were even thinking about such a reference to Mark, who had just celebrated his fortieth birthday last fall? A week ago, we had been worried only about hiccups.

In less than a week, Mark's fever resolved and his heart rate slowed, although it remained elevated. His white blood cell count edged back up to 19,000; normal is less than 10,000. He wriggled that toe! This was news! But then he went back to sleep again.

On September 23, Mark opened his eyes a little bit, but did not focus. A heart ECHO came back normal as did Doppler exams of the right and left carotid arteries in his neck, both of which branch off the aorta. That meant that Dr. Baptiste's Cath Lab handiwork was intact and functioning well. We were hopeful with these few signs of improvement.

The days dragged. Mark remained comatose, except for a few weak but unpurposeful movements. Sedatives were decreased so he could more easily respond. The whole family thought of ways to stimulate Mark. A Texas A&M shirt was brought in, which normally would have elicited a scornful snort from this UT grad; his nieces thumped his forehead with their fingers, hoping for at least some reaction, but they were only rewarded with a tiny head movement. Football games roared on the TV, music played, but Mark slept on.

When we all went to church the Sunday following Mark's surgery, the entire congregation prayed for Mark. Their support was overwhelming. On the way home, Tabor said, "I'll love Daddy even if he's in a wheelchair...in fact, I've always wanted to try out a wheelchair myself."

Nancy, Carol, and I snickered a little. Marshall was not to be outdone, though.

"I'll love Daddy even if he has Band-Aids all over his whole body."

Despite our overall downheartedness, we actually laughed. It felt good.

Back at the hospital, we were told that Mark's body was fighting the infection. One or two different bacteria are common in a severe infection, but in Mark's case, five culprits were identified, along with Candida albicans, or yeast. Some of the bacteria were expected: Group C Streptococcus, common orally; Pseudomonas aeruginosa, often found in very ill people; Lactobacillus from yogurt, which Nancy had been pushing Mark to eat. But there were also two esoteric bacteria: Actinomyces israelii and Finegoldia magna. His infectious disease specialist repeatedly fine-tuned his antibiotics to "fit the drugs to the bugs", in medical parlance.

After a day or two, a few of his vital signs started to show some hint of improvement. Immediately after surgery Mark had been put on several medications to keep his dangerously low blood pressure from cratering, but as the days went on, he needed less of them and finally none at all. His blood values showed fewer signs of the trauma he had been through as the days wore slowly on. But Mark still showed no signs of awakening.

After post-op day three, it felt like Mark had lain in Room 5 for weeks. He was weaned off all sedatives to help him wake up more quickly. All the while, a continual bedside vigil of family and friends continued. His parents, sisters, and their families kept constant watch. We talked to him, prayed individually, and even prayed together, holding hands with friends and church members circled around his bed. Nancy brought in his favorite music. Nieces came home from college, his sister-in-law had flown in from Boston, attendants from his and Nancy's wedding drove or flew in, people from work dropped in, and families of Tabor's and Marshall's schoolmates and teachers came by with snacks and meals.

Time continued to creep at an abysmally slow pace. Nothing was happening. As far as his responding to our touch, voices, jokes, songs, music, notes, and the kids' artwork…he just didn't. The family took turns spending the night in Room 5, but the morning report remained the same as the night report: no change.

Tabor and Marshall were curious and wanted to see Mark, but they were understandably reluctant. Nancy wanted them involved, too, but was unsure how to approach the situation. She had enrolled them in Wonders and Worries, a free service in Austin. There, they met with counselors and other children who had parents who were severely ill, so they had had a bit of an introduction into the situation in Room 5.

Yet here lay their father: non-responsive, unmoving, hooked up to all kinds of noisy and scary gadgets, unable to acknowledge their presence, dressed in a hospital gown, not his usual tee shirt and shorts. Mark had always assumed the role of protector, the ultimate care-giver for his family. How do you introduce this traumatic vision to his children? He and Nancy had always insisted on protecting the kids from the word cancer; this was much worse, much more hopeless, and so much uglier. Nancy couldn't get Mark's opinion on what to do now; she had to act for both. She decided to face it head-on. After all, she'd be right there with them.

The ICU nurses helped Nancy with baby steps for Marshall and Tabor to be reintroduced to their father who was still on life support, with three left-sided chest tubes, another tube going into his abdominal wall, a complex tangle of multiple IVs, the ostomy bag on his left neck, bags hanging from the bedside with green or yellow contents, the cacophony of bells and warnings with digital readouts of vital signs snaking across the monitor above his head.

First, they led the children along with Nancy out of the ICU waiting room through the locked door to the unit, then later walked with them down the hall, then into Room 5, and finally behind the curtain to Mark's bedside. Thanks to the nurses' patience and caring, the children responded very well, accepting what they saw. They seemed to absorb the situation more with curiosity than horror. They even managed to pose by his bedside with Nancy for a family picture.

After that long period of near non-responsiveness, gradually, gradually, there were changes in Mark. Tiny, subtle changes at first: an eye twitch when spoken to, a response to a squeeze of a toe. The blue big toe began to pink up. His vital signs came closer to acceptable, though still abnormal. Then he started to open his eyes when spoken to, then track with his eyes. The goal was for Mark to be able to communicate and follow directions enough to be weaned off the ventilator. The date was September 24, five days post-surgery.

This was both overwhelmingly joyful for Nancy but scary too. Was Mark still Mark? Where had his mind been since he had endured the Cardiac Cath lab maneuvers? What would he say? Would those six septic embolic strokes, although small, have affected his speech or movements? Would he even know her? Was he the same man who had told her just recently that he wanted to grow old with her?

There were other concerns, too. Mark's white blood cell count (WBC) was now 26,000, nearly three times normal, despite huge doses of multiple IV antibiotics and constant irrigation of the chest cavity with more high-powered antimicrobials. Thus, the elevated WBC indicated he wasn't adequately fighting the chest infection. His ID doctor increased the antibiotic dosages, telling Nancy that the aortic graft would always be infected; Mark would be on antibiotics continuously until the graft could be replaced. The doctor then joined us in prayer in Room 5.

Mark finally seemed to respond to the new dosages. He squeezed Nancy's hand to the point that it hurt. But later, his WBC increased to 30,000, then later still, 34,000. IV antibiotics were changed again and increased. The chest tube irrigation cocktail was stopped, since it seemed not to be helpful. He began to breathe a bit on his own. Although still on the ventilator, his breathing pace, initiation of breaths, and oxygen became normal. His pulmonary doctor introduced the idea of extubation, or taking him off the ventilator. When Dr. Baptiste made rounds, Nancy asked him where to direct our prayers; he replied, "That massive chest infection needs to cease and desist."

Six days post-op, a tracheostomy tube was being considered since Mark had been intubated for so long. This would involve making an incision in the front of his neck and hooking up the ventilator from there, thus freeing up his mouth while still protecting his airway. Eventually, when he could breathe entirely on his own, that trache tube could be removed. Physical therapy had started by passively moving Mark's limbs; speech and occupational therapy waited in the wings.

The next day, visitors were restricted to family only; Mark needed to rest, because he had been restless all night long. Hiccups recurred. But his WBC was down to 30,000 again, and his weaning parameters for achieving removal from the ventilator were improving rapidly. At long last, late in the afternoon, he could cooperate enough that the tube was removed. Nancy held her breath; tears of joy rolled down her face. Mark was breathing on his own. Now what?

Mark took one look at Nancy and said, "I love you."

She, of course, was ecstatic, and sobbed in relief.

After being in ICU for so long, patients often experience some disorientation, and Mark's case was no exception. His mentation was, at first, a bit scrambled; he'd get confused. Introduced for the first time to Dr. Baptiste, Mark stared awhile at this doctor he had never met, who had done surgery on him twice, who had saved his life. Then he spoke, "You're a cop!"

Nancy was amused but totally perplexed. Where that had come from? Dr. Baptiste just smiled at Mark's outburst and said his brother was a detective in Houston but that he, for sure, was not. Mark had no previous knowledge of any of that. As Nancy continued with the introductions, Mark slowly realized that Dr. Baptiste had, indeed, saved his life. He sat up in bed: the first significant movement in ten days, offering a handshake. Just a few days before, he had been unable to react to even the most noxious stimulus; with much adjusting still to do, Mark was starting on his way back.

The next day was difficult; fluid was filling his one remaining lung, making breathing difficult. Three liters were pulled off the lung by diuretics. His WBC went back up to 34,000. He was still confused sometimes, even agitated on occasion. We were reassured that this was normal. The plan was to remove the left upper chest tubes after filling the lung cavity one last time with the final antibiotic cocktail.

Despite the seriousness of the situation, some things were even comical; in his post-extubation confusion, Mark at one point grumbled to Nancy, "Bring me my wallet. Let's check out of this hotel. I don't like it here."

CHAPTER 21

• • •

ON SEPTEMBER 29, MARK WAS taken for his first ride out of ICU Room 5 by wheelchair. He was thrilled. He was even able to sit up for six minutes. His nasal oxygen prongs were removed; his oxygen saturation of the right lung was normal now that the fluid was gone. On Day 14 of ICU, Mark twice stood by his bed.

The stay in ICU after he was off the ventilator went slowly, but as he progressed, his medications were decreased except for his antibiotics. Mark's spirits were high; his sense of humor returned.

By October 1, his WBC decreased to 24,000; although far from normal, the cell count was at least heading in the right direction. His feedings, pumped thorough the J port of the GJ-tube, were begun at a snail's pace to prevent abdominal pain and diarrhea. Because of its small caliber, the J port was easily clogged with crushed medications; suctioning, adding diet soda or warm water, and at times a little silent prayer, opened it once again. Nancy took notes, preparing for when she would be in charge at home. This particular tube, although necessary in Mark's complex case, caused all sorts of issues, because everyone was so unfamiliar and uncomfortable using it to give nutrition and oral medications to Mark.

The G-tube port of the GJ-tube had been used since surgery specifically to suction bile out of Mark's non-functioning stomach. Eventually, suction was no longer needed, and the G-tube port was capped off until it would be needed months later for direct stomach feeding. Despite all the best efforts including earlier TPN and now J-tube port feedings, Mark was still severely malnourished. His prealbumin, a lab value that indicates nutritional well-being, was merely half would it should be. The hospital nutritionist tweaked his caloric intake to give his body the energy needed both to heal and to feel better. He now weighed only around 145 pounds, down from his usual 200 pounds on his 6'3" frame.

Being fed by the J port of the GJ-tube, Mark was not actually hungry, but his physical therapists stressed the importance of keeping the facial muscles active by chewing. Everything he ate went into the small ostomy bag on the left of his neck. It could hold about a soda canful. At this early point, he had no oral intake.

October 2 arrived; his WBC was now down to 15,800. Physical therapy had him doing hourly exercises. On October 3, he was moved out of ICU, no longer considered critical. His new home was the Intermediate Care Unit or IMCU. Just two days later, his WBC normalized at 9,000. There had been a bit of a scare with Pseudomonas aeruginosa infection again, involving the feeding tube, but a visit to IR or Interventional Radiology and changes in antibiotics had taken care of it. IR is a specialty unto itself, using tiny catheters and other instruments to get into the distant nooks and crannies of the body where normal instruments can't reach.

Just as in dealing with the unfamiliarity of the GJ-tube, the same situation occurred when it came to dealing with the esophageal ostomy bag. The most common refrain from Mark's nurses was, "I've never seen one of these before." But they had a willingness to learn; it became a daily routine of trial and error with various styles of bags, adhesives, and skin hygiene products.

Nancy watched with an eagle eye. She invested in the challenge right away, since she knew it would eventually fall to her to deal with the bag, its care, and its application after Mark returned home. She talked to and met with various wound care specialists both in and out of the hospital, taking notes on their favorite ostomy care ideas, which were few since an ostomy bag on a neck was highly unusual. Adding to the problem was Mark's fifty-five-pound weight loss; his neck was simply so skinny above his collarbone, there were too many hills and valleys to hold a bag. When it began to fill, Nancy was quick to empty it; as it got heavy, the bag would pull on and irritate his skin or fall off altogether. The bags cost $8.00 each, lasted only three days at most, and were not readily available; these issues added to the challenge. For every trial, it seemed there would be two or more errors.

During this time in IMCU recovery, physical therapy was vigorously employed. Passive movements of Mark's limbs continued, but now it was up to Mark's body to relearn how to strengthen his weak muscles. The physical therapists got him up and moving as much as possible.

Mark gradually, with help, increased his activity—bed to chair, then later to the bathroom, still connected by his IVs and GJ-tube on a pump. He didn't like the pump at all; it kept him awake at night, as it needed to run twenty-four hours a day to intensify his nutrition. He learned to tolerate it but was never able to ignore it completely. The speed of the pump was still at a trickle and would be increased as his body was more able to tolerate it.

IMCU was a much more comfortable place than the ICU, though.

"When can I start eating?"

His nurse checked his orders. "Now! What do you want?"

He wasn't sure since he wasn't hungry, so his nurse suggested a Popsicle. I was there when he ate it; his face beamed like he had reached Nirvana.

"That's the best tasting thing I've ever had in my life!"

But the contents of his ostomy bag suspended from his left neck felt uncomfortably cold; not entirely unexpected, since his esophagus was now only a few inches long and surgically tunneled through his neck tissues and connected to the small bag.

We switched to lollipops and what had been his favorite drink for years: Dublin sodas made in Dublin, Texas, and carried only by a few area stores. We dragged them by bagsful into his IMCU room. A nurse asked Mark which flavor was his favorite.

"All of them."

Later in his stay, after passing his swallowing tests, he could chew up and swallow anything, since the chewed-up food went directly into the bag. No nutrition entered his bloodstream, of course. Because each bag had a trapdoor in its bottom, the same bag could remain for a few days. We learned how to empty the contents into a plastic container and then flush it away.

Soon Mark inquired if he could have his bed turned ninety degrees to look out the window. He told the nurses, "If you stay in the bed all the time, the view is always the same."

This was great news, for his doctors encouraged him to be more independent, a healthy sign. Because of electrical and other hookups for the bed, however, his request was denied, but we moved the heavy side chair so he could look out the window when he sat in it. When we did so, he grinned wryly, "Wow! Now I can look right into my primary care doctor's parking lot."

This was the quick wit of the Mark we knew and loved.

Mark was still quite weak but could get around a bit with assistance. He could watch a football game and understand what was going on. Friends, co-workers, and family continued to visit, as if to witness this miracle themselves. His room was usually full of St. David's well-wishers. Hospital employees who had assisted in his initial resuscitation in the ER, Cath Lab, and OR came by to cheer him on. Hospital executives, aides, and custodians did too. One of his nurses was on the same kickball team as his sister Kellye. He became a sort of celebrity by surviving and indeed thriving despite the enormous physical and psychological trauma he had undergone. Each spoke the same mantra, "You are a miracle!"

Many visited with tears in their eyes. Wade told him in a tender moment how much he admired his son. "I could not have so nobly done what you did." At one point, I overheard Wade say to Mark as he helped untangle his IV lines at the bedside, "Thank you for allowing me to feel useful."

Elaine became the foot-rub specialist; she had the knack for helping him deal with stiffness and his old chemo-induced nagging pain. Because it was early October, all visitors had to have had a flu shot. Since kids have the highest incidence of viral infection, no children, including his own, were allowed for a while.

On October 7, a deep vein thrombosis or clot, was found in Mark's neck and had to be treated with twice-daily shots. He was eventually taken for walks; physical therapists taught Nancy how to walk closely behind Mark with a wheelchair while they supported him and helped with his IV pole and walker. The distances grew from just a few feet to down the hall. This exercise was exhausting and painful, but he gritted his teeth and went on. On October 9, with his walker, Mark travelled thirty feet. He was sleeping well, too. He said he wanted to remain at St. David's at Round Rock for rehab when the time came.

On October 11, Mark walked 100 feet. He could now change from sitting to lying to standing with little assistance. He wanted to eat more; undergoing further swallowing tests, he passed them all. His pulmonologist stressed that aspiration of food into his remaining lung would be devastating. He was not allowed to lie flat, probably ever again. Physical, speech, and occupational therapies advanced their work with Mark.

His speech was now clear and coherent. Still, however, his doctors ordered speech therapy to exercise his facial muscles; one morning I witnessed one of his speech sessions.

Mark was cooperative but enjoyed having a bit of fun at the speech therapist's expense. Ordered to say as many words as he could think of that began with the letter F, he began with the obvious ones: "four, finger, funny;" she signaled to him to continue. Then he smiled at her and shook his head slightly, as if to say "no naughty words!" Instead, he said "fractal" and "felonious," just to show off. I had to laugh; Mark's sense of humor was healing too.

His mentation was totally intact. After that short initial post-extubating fog, he became his usual smiling, intelligent, and at times ornery self. He liked to watch his beloved UT Longhorns; family and friends would join him until he became worn out and needed to rest. Nancy brought his laptop and other electronic toys to pass the time.

We began to talk about what to do when he got out of the hospital. This prompted us to search the availability of wedge pillows, shims, back "systems" to help keep Mark's head elevated after he went home.

Nancy, of course, had been taking notes from the very beginning. She watched the nurses change dressings, set up J-port tube feedings, and change the ostomy bag. She doggedly observed, videoed, questioned, requested ideas on how to handle feedings, crush medicines, liquefy powders, and unplug the J part of the feeding tube when it became clogged. She asked for advice on where to get IV poles for the feedings, shower chairs, how to get Mark into and out of bed, where to put the hospital bed he would need for his return home. And on and on and on.

Never had she ever had to do this in her life. She correctly mused that it would be sort of like bringing a newborn home: there was just no instructional manual; even with help from home health personnel, she would have to figure everything out as it came along.

As Mark's condition improved, he was frequently reminded by his medical team: his job now was to get as healthy as he could. This was to prepare him for future surgeries in Houston to replace the aortic graft and to reconstruct and reattach his esophagus. These surgeries would be intricate, invasive, and major.

CHAPTER 22

• • •

ON OCTOBER 14, NEARLY A month after admission, Mark was clinically ready for discharge to a skilled nursing facility or SNF, pronounced "sniff." He was not happy; he was not a candidate for the rehab unit at St. David's, so he wanted to be at home. But, his doctors reasoned, he would still need lots of care for his various tubes, surgical dressing changes, physical therapy and help with recovering to get ready for Houston. He was told that only time would tell, but that December or January might be a surgical goal if all went well.

Nancy toured the choices available. The closest fit was less than optimal since the SNF was in the heart of Austin, difficult to get to with two young children in school in the northwest area of the city. Mark, resigned to being denied his choice, was sent by ambulance.

There was trouble right away. This was not an acute care facility. It was a place to prepare for home discharge; the pace was much slower here. Mark, of course, wanted to "get on it" concerning his rehab, impatient with how time-consuming it would be for the staff to learn about his unique and complex care.

Staff at the SNF were more familiar with caring for older patients with strokes and post-orthopedic patients with knee or hip replacements, not a forty-year-old eager to escape institutional living and go home. Mark's admitting diagnosis was officially "severe debilitation and deconditioning needing treatment with inpatient PT/OT". Sounds simple enough, but Mark's unusual devices and surgical and medical history presented huge hurdles for his caregivers. As expected, just the presence of the GJ-tube was perplexing and foreign. Although the two upper chest tubes had been removed, the lower back chest tube remained. It still needed suction and daily attention. Emptying the ostomy bag above his left collar bone after meals was a totally alien task to staff members. They were just as unfamiliar with the process as his earlier staff at St. David's had been. The chorus of *"I've never worked with this before"* chafed at us, even though we had been prepared to hear it.

Although Mark no longer had an active blood-stream infection, and his labs were nearly normal, he still needed round-the-clock care. Just to get him up walking again was difficult; here was a 6'3" man, now weighing only 142 pounds, nearly sixty pounds lighter than normal. He was still weak and needed assistance getting around. He was also still on IV antibiotics, and his feedings into the J-port were on a pump, 24/7. The gastric part of the GJ-tube was capped off and the stomach bypassed, just as at the hospital. The staff had to learn how to handle this foreign gadget.

As each day at the SNF passed, Mark became increasingly frustrated. Here was an intelligent high-powered man who wanted to move along quickly in his healing and rehab; his spirit was undaunted but his body had taken such a beating that his progress was maddeningly slow. He continued pleading for release from the SNF. His mantra was, "I want out of here!"

Be careful what you wish for. Mark did, in fact, leave that facility after just six days, but not to go home.

CHAPTER 23

• • •

It was a Sunday morning at the SNF, and as Mark's usual medications were being put into his J-tube port, it became clogged. All the normal measures failed to clear it. I happened to be sitting in his room as the staff wrangled with the obstruction.

All at once I heard Mark's voice loud and clear, "I am so upset by what I just saw!"

I shot out of my chair to look; there was the far end of the tube, dripping with liquefied formula and ground-up pills, lying on his abdomen, completely out of the stoma it had been sewn into. Thus, all his nutrition, medications, and fluids would now be unavailable to him. A flurry of activity and long-winded phone calls followed, but finally a consensus was reached: Mark would have to be readmitted to St. David's for tube replacement. Two hours later, he left by ambulance.

Mark felt right at home back at St. David's despite not wanting to be in a hospital at all. It was the next best thing to being home. All the ER staff recognized him as the celebrity patient who had recently cheated death at their facility. Over and over he would hear, "You again? Did you miss us? You sure look better than the last time you came in here."

After having his GJ-tube replaced in Interventional Radiology, Mark was admitted directly to the oncology floor. He was happy there since he was almost home, no longer in ICU or IMCU. He could see his usual doctors, and his care continued. Although in pain often, he declined narcotics in favor of over-the-counter meds. He referred to this as his pain management strategy: wanting to be mentally awake and alert, he'd work through the pain to take his mind off it.

The good news was that he was not considered septic; his antibiotic regimen was simplified, and the chest tube was no longer attached to suction. This was an upgrade for him. It took a few days to stabilize his blood pressure and blood sugars. On October 22, he could walk up and down the hall without a cane or a walker. He was even cleared to use stairs once a day after going home. He was almost ready to be discharged. This time the discharge destination was actually home. Just four days after this latest admission to St. David's, Mark was discharged.

At the house on Grapevine Lane, there was much preparation work and social services at the hospital were wonderful in helping with the transition home. But something as simple as getting a hospital bed, for example, became another nightmare. First, there must be an appointment to have it delivered when an adult would be present. Then, where do you put it? Nancy decided the best place for Mark would be their upstairs bedroom since he still spent quite a bit of time in bed. There'd be the nearby bathroom, too.

Kellye and I were there when they delivered the bed. It looked too small for a 6'3" man; we measured it: no good; it was nearly five inches too short, especially for a tall man in a head's up position; Mark would always be scooting out of it. So back it went, and a longer bed was delivered, but the mattress was small and thin. Since it was now late in the day, we accepted it, then added a mattress from Marshall's trundle bed to give it some thickness.

Tabor and Marshall had balloons up throughout the house and a *Welcome Home* sign in the front yard. Nancy picked up Mark at the hospital in the minivan. The kids and I welcomed him out front while Baxter and Beau barked and circled around. Relying on Nancy's support, Mark insisted on walking into the house despite feeling weak. He made it to the couch where Nancy, Tabor, Marshall and then Baxter and Beau welcomed him home. He could not stop smiling.

That night Mark slept in the hospital bed at the foot of their king-size bed. It was a rough night; the next morning he banished the hospital bed and announced he'd sleep in his own wonderful bed from then on. And that's the way it was. Mark was truly home.

Since Mark's admission on September 16, friends continued to provide dinner three times weekly at the Grapevine Lane home. Each would bring a meal to the house, leaving it in a cooler on the porch. All we had to do then was heat and serve. This would continue for many months; at times the meal would be home-cooked; sometimes, it came from a restaurant or was given as a gift card. Early on, we carefully listed each donor and meal; soon, though, we lost track. Even the children's teachers took turns making the kids brown bag lunches. Each meal was considered a godsend; we knew we'd never be able to express adequate thanks.

The biggest challenge was to learn how to care for all of Mark's issues: checking blood pressures and blood sugars, giving a blood-thinning injection every twelve hours, preparing medications, setting up feeding bags and dealing with the noisy and irritating pump and GJ-tube, making sure the chest tube remained patent. Nancy spent hours looking online for the best and most economical ostomy bags; she even tried a pediatric urine bag since the opening on Mark's neck was so small. She met with vendors to obtain sample bags to try.

It took a while to get into a routine: the kitchen was designated as the food and medicine station. First, Mark had six pills to take twice a day. These, of course, had to be crushed and given via the J-tube port—his stomach was still not functioning. Nancy had photographed the hospital's professional pill crusher and ordered it online. She pulverized each pill separately in a tiny plastic sleeve, heated 200 cc of water for exactly twenty seconds: too hot would melt the plastic; too cold would not dissolve the crushed pills. Then she added the water and stirred with a dull plastic knife. She had been told not to combine all six mixtures; that would increase the risk of a clog in the small-caliber J-tube port. Then she had to get all six doses upstairs without a spill.

At first, she juggled the tiny containers; in short order, though, she discovered it was easier just to place each sleeve in a compartment of a muffin tin. Upstairs, she then had to stop the continuous tube feeding, or the pump would continue on, shooting the formula everywhere. She learned this the hard way: it was a sticky mess that only the dogs enjoyed. Then, after opening only the J-port, she attached a large syringe with the plunger removed. Next, she slowly dumped each sleeve's contents, followed by a warm-water rinse, into the syringe. Too much, too fast, too hot, or too cold all caused abdominal discomfort. Finally, the remainder of the 200 cc of water were very slowly added to the J-tube port to keep it from clogging.

Some medications were not meant for crushing, so substitutes had to be found. Some liquids were so sticky that they adhered to the inside of the tube which at times could not be cleared. A clog was to be prevented at all costs, but sometimes it happened anyway and had to be dealt with. Unclogging the tube was just as harrowing for her as it had been for the nurses at the hospital. The whole medication process took at least thirty minutes in the beginning but became shorter as she got into the groove. It was absolutely imperative that the J port, not the G port, of the tube be used; Mark's stomach was still non-functional.

Then there were the feedings themselves to deal with. The tube feeding formula ran continuously via a noisy pump that Mark loathed. Nancy searched online and eventually found a quieter model. The nutritionist at the hospital had calculated exactly how much formula Mark needed every twenty-four hours. The real trick was to figure out how to get that into him without causing abdominal cramps or diarrhea. First, she found that squeezing air out of the bag after filling it was helpful. Then there was dealing with the speed of the pump. It was a sort of double-edged sword. If Nancy dripped the formula faster, she ran the risk of those side-effects. If she slowed down, and Mark received less than the required calories, he'd impede his weight gain. It was truly a trial and error system with Mark's tolerability calling the shots.

There was also "the dance of the bag" Nancy learned; like giving medications, this involved stopping the pump to refill the bag, opening and closing the correct ports and clamps, closing the tube at just the right time to avoid spills. The first few times a spill occurred, both dogs thought they had won the lottery. They made a bee-line for the liquid food puddle on the floor and lapped gleefully as we tried to clean it up. Other times they would get tangled up in the tubing if Mark were lying on the couch. Nancy had designated an array of dishtowels and old baby washcloths for just such occurrences.

Then there were issues with the formula; at first several cases were sent by UPS, which Nancy would find out later was a luxury they couldn't long afford. She and the kids became so familiar with the UPS man, Tony Rivas, that the children would answer the door bell, yelling, "Mom, it's Tony!"

Nancy would come to the door and Tony would deliver the heavy cases, digging dog treats out of his pockets for Baxter and Beau, "Hey, Mrs. C. How are ya? How's Mr. C?" It was always considered a break to hear his laugh and exchange a few words.

When cost forced her to change strategy, Nancy found the solution online; indeed, it cost less but was maddeningly cumbersome. She would have to calculate how much tube feeding to order, how often, and exactly when she could pick it up twenty minutes away. Then there were issues with formula that had spoiled. It became an art, figuring out if a case was acceptable or not. Nancy would mark a can from a new case before giving it to Mark. If it curdled in the bag or if he had digestion problems, she would have to drive the whole case back to exchange it. There was no way to predict this; expiration dates were unhelpful; older cans would often still be good but a new case could cause cramping or diarrhea. When a case finally passed muster, all cans from it were placed in a kitchen cabinet, safe to use.

Another issue to deal with: expensive feeding bags, tubing, and ostomy bags were sent home with Mark from the hospital. When we considered the cost of bags for pump feeding, we were shocked. We had been told that the expensive continuous feedings would not be forever; when Mark started to gain back his weight, we could switch to the cheaper ordinary IV bags and let the formula drain in by gravity. Nancy did find some cheaper pump bags, but it was still a huge albeit necessary expense.

The ostomy bags were a different story. These cost even more since they were so esoteric. She tried a variety of bags, different sizes and types of adhesive skin connection systems, different types of drainage openings so the bag could be emptied after he ate. There were choices of protective skin products, specialized skin wipes, and different maneuvers to help keep the bag on for longer periods. Although she had learned all she could at the hospital, Nancy realized it was going to be just another problem to solve while at home.

Because Mark was so weak, at first Nancy had to get into the shower with him and a shower chair, taking care not to dislodge the ostomy bag, the GJ-tube or the one remaining chest tube. If it were a day for a bag change, she would disconnect it just before showering to ease washing Mark's skin at the ostomy site. Once out of the shower, the ostomy, minus the bag, had to be covered with a gauze pad, since saliva is produced continuously and would drip down Mark's clean chest. It became routine to hear Nancy say, "Don't swallow!" as she prepped his skin to reattach the bag.

Of course, there was help from insurance and visiting nurses, but we were amazed at how much insurance did not cover, due to Mark's special medical equipment and supply needs. Visiting nurses came and went, not surprisingly unfamiliar with Mark's GJ-tube, ostomy bags and chest tube. Some nurses were not allowed to deal directly with tube or ostomy problems, because they were not RNs. Yet even when the RNs did come, we heard the old familiar refrain, "I've never seen anything like this before." It got to be easier for Nancy just to figure it out on her own.

So, she did. Over and over again. She kept detailed daily timelines in a notebook. Complete medication lists hung on the inside of the kitchen cabinets. Syringes and other medical paraphernalia all had their respective places in bins on the kitchen counter. Near the entrance of their master bedroom, she retrofitted a DVD cabinet to become her own personal medical office, complete with BP cuff, glucose meter, professional thermometer, and oximeter, to name a few, plus a myriad of medical supplies from latex gloves to sterile gauze pads.

CHAPTER 24

• • •

JUST SIX DAYS AFTER HIS coming home, Nancy had to take Mark back to St. David's ER. By then Mark was moving around the house quite well, but that morning, his one remaining chest tube had fallen out from his lower left back. Since the left chest cavity was still draining pus-contaminated fluid, the tube had to be replaced. With the help of his primary care doctor, Mark was worked in at St. David's interventional radiology or IR department; because he was unscheduled; however, it turned into an all-day affair.

It had turned cold, and Mark was miserable with discomfort; although Nancy had taken warm clothes, feeding formula, and blankets, she hadn't realized the length of time it would take and didn't include his pain medication. The radiologist in the IR department replaced the chest tube late in the afternoon. The only positive aspect of the uncomfortable day was that so many staff at the hospital again recognized Mark, going out of their way to help make him and Nancy comfortable.

They surely didn't feel very comfortable at that point. Somehow, though, they made it through a very long day and were home shortly after the kids got home from school. Both were exhausted. As soon as she walked in the door, Nancy packed a small bottle of pain meds into Mark's back-to-the-hospital bag. She would be ready for any future ER visits.

And there were plenty of those visits. Nancy had to transport Mark several times to the ER for interventional radiology to reopen or replace the GJ-tube because of clogging. That back-to-the-hospital bag remained by the door. Too many times the J-tube port would refuse to unclog despite pushing warm water or carbonated beverages through. Everyone seemed to have an idea including nursing staff, an RN family member, the internet, the GJ-tube manufacturer itself. It still clogged.

It was almost November; cooler temperatures awakened discussions about Thanksgiving. It would be different this year, but at least they were all together at home. Mark's fevers would come and go, and life went on, getting back to normal. His short-term goal was to be up and around and feeling better for Thanksgiving.

This was a time of year he loved. Thanksgiving meant a long weekend with everyone going to his parents' ranch in Paint Rock, having a big family get-together and feast, and going hunting with his brothers-in-law and his father. He knew he'd have to curtail the hunting, but he eagerly looked forward to it just the same. That train of thought lasted only two days, however.

CHAPTER 25

• • •

NOVEMBER 2013

ON NOVEMBER 2, MARK DEVELOPED fever and chills; his blood pressure dropped and he could barely get out of bed. Nancy drove him back at St. David's, and Mark was readmitted emergently to ICMU for reassessment, a change in IV antibiotics, and other tests to see what had caused this. We assumed it would be a short in-and-out admission since he had been on antibiotics the entire time he had been home. We were wrong.

This time, Mark had to stay in the hospital for ten days. His primary diagnosis turned out to be recurrent sepsis stemming from the original aortic graft. Blood cultures showed that not all five bacteria had resolved after all. Pseudomonas aeruginosa, common in people in poor health, had managed to evade all the antibiotics he'd received. New IV and GJ-tube antimicrobials were introduced; as before, the new medications clogged his J tube port and the reopening drill started again. Nancy kept a sharp eye on that tube; since it clogged at the hospital, it would do the same at home. Multiple adjustments eventually restored the J-tube port patency.

Another diagnosis was protein-calorie malnutrition; translated: starvation. Despite everyone's best efforts, Mark was unable to dig himself out of his fifty-pound weight loss. He had a certain style of Levi jeans that he loved; I returned pair after pair to get him a size that wasn't too big. His feedings were increased to the highest calorie count possible, with the pump running as fast as his body could tolerate.

Physical therapy worked to get him moving more, and gradually he started to feel better. His echocardiogram was normal. The goal remained the same: get healthy enough to go to Houston to have the aortic graft replaced and the esophagus repaired and reattached.

During this hospitalization, Mark celebrated his forty-first birthday. The entire family came; Elaine brought a huge 41-shaped balloon bouquet. There were cake and ice cream, laughter, and song. Lots of visitors came over the ten-day hospitalization; his sisters and their families arrived for watching ballgames on TV. Wade and Elaine were there lending their support. While hospitalized, Mark read the entire biography of Steve Jobs. Eventually he could walk again, slowly and unsteadily all the way around the unit as long as one of us accompanied him. He was discharged on November 12, 2013.

CHAPTER 26

• • •

AGAIN AT HOME, MARK CONTINUED to stay as active as possible, tolerating his pain without narcotics. The rate of his J-tube port feedings was increased slowly. By phone with his future Houston doctors, the question was framed: when is an optimal time to do those surgeries? They noted it would have to be in three parts, all of which were serious, complex, one-of-a-kind. It would have to be done in Houston, and he and Nancy would have to have an office visit with both of the doctors before it could even be scheduled. The doctors were Dr. Anthony Estrera, thoracic and cardiac surgeon and Dr. Kamal Khalil, thoracic and esophageal surgeon.

Mark and Nancy thought it through repeatedly, weighing the pros and cons. Mark's biggest physical annoyance was the esophageal ostomy; it was inconvenient, messy, and had to be fiddled with daily. It was a pain trying out different adhesives, not tearing the bag off when getting dressed, and emptying it without drawing attention to it.

Going out to eat was impossible, because anyone witnessing what they had to go through at every meal, might be appalled. The few times they had tried, it required so much planning; Nancy had to pack a bag containing extra ostomies, large opaque cups and tops to catch and then seal his chewed-up meals. Seating by the restroom was necessary for inconspicuous bag-emptying. One time, his bag pulled away from his skin while they were eating; the bag's contents filled the inside of his shirt, and the mess was unimaginable. Eventually they just gave up and ate in. In fact, the first time Mark had been strong enough to eat at the home dinner table, Marshall, eyes aghast at seeing the food filling the bag, spouted, "I love you, Daddy, but I am about to lose my dinner."

Nancy popped up and tied a large red-checkered napkin around the bag, laughing, and saying to Mark, "You're a cowboy now."

Marshall referred to the bag's contents as "Dad's chew-food." It was no wonder that Mark's recurring demand was, "I want this bag gone!"

But he was well-aware that the aortic graft was the more serious issue, of course. This created even more discussion; should the surgeries be done before Christmas and run the risk of complications that would ruin the holidays? Yet perhaps going that soon could give him an edge. If he waited, which was just not Mark's style, when would be the earliest it could be done? I overheard him say one day late that fall, "It's just weird trying so hard to get ready for three surgeries, any one of which could kill me." *True.*

It took weeks to arrange an appointment with the two Houston surgeons. After all, neither of his surgeons-to-be had ever met him, despite being familiar with his case via phone with Dr. Baptiste. After multiple phone calls, Nancy at last nailed down the dual doctor appointments.

But how to get Mark there? Memorial Hermann Texas Medical Center in Houston is about three hours from Austin, in good traffic. Should Nancy just put him in her seven-year-old minivan and go? What if it broke down? What if she got delayed and missed one or both appointments? Who should go with her? Who should stay at home with the kids? How would she rig up his feeding pump? Could he sit still that long in the van with the chest tube draining out of his side, rubbing on the seat? Family members offered their large SUVs, suggesting Marshall's mattress in the back would allow Mark to lie down. Good idea, but all the other problems still existed. Mark declined.

Nancy readied for battle. Contacting their insurance company, querying ambulance companies, verifying the visit date and times, she was promptly told that insurance did not cover non-emergent ambulance rides. They didn't realize with whom they were dealing.

I vividly recall two-year-old Nancy, after a large snowfall in Peoria, Illinois, decided she wanted some candy. I told her no. A short while later,

I felt a draft. I noticed a chair pulled over to the open coat closet. Her orange flowered parka was gone, and so was she, leaving the door ajar. Just then, I noticed colorful movement outside the window. There was Nancy, knee-deep in the snow, heading next door, the source of the neighborhood bottomless candy bowl. Her parka was on upside down, the hood hanging between her knees, but she was on a quest. This girl just never gave up on anything she set her mind to, and the adult had not changed.

It took a multitude of phone calls to many people, but Nancy pled Mark's case. The outcome: her and Mark's Houston ambulance ride would be covered. So, on November 21, the ambulance arrived at Grapevine Lane, en route to Houston.

If you have ever ridden in an ambulance, you are well aware it is not comfortable. The ride is bumpy and rigid. Any conversation requires near-shouting. Ambulances just aren't designed to take a patient for a three-hour ride, but that's what Mark and Nancy had to deal with. Yet they were both glad they were in an ambulance, where professionals could deal with Mark's issues. First, he could lie down completely—his 6'3" frame would not have fit into any conventional vehicle. He was wrapped in warm blankets; without any spare body fat, he was always cold. Strapped into a harness in the back with Mark, Nancy chatted as best she could with their attendant; Mark, not his usual wise-cracking self, was mostly silent. Since she was not directly responsible for his care en route, Nancy relaxed a bit, until Mark shouted, "I'm leaking!"

His J-tube port had disconnected; formula feeding had soaked his clothes and blankets and formed congealing pools on the floor. *Welcome to my world*, Nancy thought. At least the dogs weren't there adding to the mayhem.

Once they arrived, after a long period of waiting, Mark was finally able to see both doctors in the same office. They told him that at least another month would be necessary, because he had remained very deconditioned and had just gotten out of his third hospitalization in two months. He still had much healing to do, and the upcoming surgeries were not short, easy, or without risk. In fact, they could do only two of the three surgeries during the same hospitalization. They wanted him as fit as possible. Both surgeons had already spent a lot of time planning the surgeries, since Mark's case was basically one-of-a-kind. His cardiothoracic surgeon, Dr. Estrera, was most concerned about the infected graft; removing and replacing it was of prime importance to prevent further infection. Mark had already experienced that with the recent Pseudomonas readmission. His thoracic esophageal surgeon, Dr. Khalil, had less life-threatening issues, but he echoed Dr. Estrera's concerns, because he too would be invading the left chest cavity. The aorta would have to be in the best shape possible before he could do his work. The third and final surgery, to reattach the esophagus to the upper part now opening to the stoma, would take place a month or more after the first two.

The doctors had further input. They insisted that scheduling must be set so that they both would be available at the bedside post-op for a long stretch of time; these surgeries were so unusual and complex that if something did go wrong, it could quickly become life-threatening. Because of this, they assured Mark, they would not trust his immediate post-op care to anyone other than themselves. They shared that they had already consulted national experts on the best way to do this three-part surgery. Both reiterated that they had never seen a case like this. Mark was, once again, unique.

Since the holidays had already begun, Mark was given two dates to choose from: he could be admitted the week after Thanksgiving with surgery after the first week of December; otherwise, he'd have to wait until after the New Year.

The plan was for Dr. Estrera to insert the new aortic graft, leaving the old graft in place. Then he would do some rerouting of the aorta itself, then remove the old graft. Next, Dr. Khalil would rebuild the esophagus and deal with the chest cavity. They would work together in the OR. Finally, after a month or so, the third and last surgery would be done to get rid of the ostomy bag. Of course, Mark chafed at the delay with that third surgery, but he knew and accepted that it was of lesser importance overall, and agreed with the plan.

The trip home took far longer than the initial trip due to traffic. The three-hour trip home stretched to five hours. Mark and Nancy arrived home, worn out, cold, and uncomfortable. As they sank into bed that night, they were grateful to be back home; it had been an exhausting, unending day, but it was finally over. They could take their time, slowly think through all that the two surgeons had told them. They could relax a little. Or so they thought.

• • •

THE VERY NEXT DAY, MARK'S J-tube port became impossibly clogged again. Off they went again, back to IR at St. David's. I was amazed how much Nancy had this down to an art. Within fifteen minutes of being told to drive in, they were in the car with his emergency bag and on their way. But because this was an ER work-in, the procedure turned out to be five hours; the tube refused to unclog and thus had to be replaced totally.

They arrived home chilled, aching, totally exhausted from both the previous day's ambulance trip to Houston and that day's hour-after-hour wait in the IR department. Nancy's comment was, "Are we ever going to catch a break?" Mark wondered the same thing.

Mark's doctors and Nancy concentrated on getting him "fattened up" to be in the best shape possible for his two big surgeries. Mark's weight was still 141. All nourishment had to be by tube, but he just kept losing weight despite high-calorie formulas at the highest speed his body could safely handle. His strength did increase to the point that one day he sat in his office chair for thirty minutes; this was a new milestone. As much as Mark loved being at the computer, this took enormous energy he just didn't have; he'd have to resort to being back in bed to rest again.

By this time, Thanksgiving had arrived. The Clifton clan venue was changed to Wade and Elaine's home in Austin instead of at the ranch in Paint Rock. It felt almost like old times, with the same family members present, along with dogs, noise, conversation, and tantalizing kitchen aromas. But not for Mark.

Usually vibrant and exuberant, Mark sat huddled in Wade's recliner, covered with a blanket, while his feeding tube continued to pump. He was thin, pale, and uncharacteristically quiet. He wasn't able to eat much and had to have Nancy take him home early. We all felt sadness for his loss of health, good cheer, and optimism. As hard as everyone tried, especially Mark, it was not a good time.

Just after Thanksgiving, on December 1, Mark's parents, sisters and their families came to the house on Grapevine Lane to decorate for Christmas. Mark announced that he and Nancy had made the final decision about going to Houston: the first surgery, rebuilding and rerouting the aorta, would be in December. Several days later, the first esophageal repair would be done, and the old aortic graft would be replaced. He would be in the hospital for at least two weeks, which, on one hand, made him very sad; he and Nancy would probably miss Christmas. On the other hand, they both felt that time was of the essence; the risks of waiting seemed just too high to postpone until January. All his family agreed with the decision. A toast was made to celebrate the moment, but Mark was unable to handle even a sip.

At their house, there were forays into the attic to retrieve decorations, music, food, drink, and lots of laughter. Mark was valiant in his efforts to join in the decorating festivities, but he was capable only of lying on the couch the entire time. His body seemed unable to rally beyond merely getting around. The house did look lovely afterward, but the spirit of Christmas was absent.

A week later, Dr. Baptiste spoke with Nancy and Mark, adding his blessing to the December surgical dates. Mark's labs were nearly normal, and his chest X-ray showed a clear right lung. Mark was feeling a little better, enjoying his favorite holiday foods: Dublin sodas, chocolate, and queso. But not for long.

CHAPTER 28

• • •

ON DECEMBER 9, MARK BEGAN to run a low-grade fever. When it reached 101.7, Nancy took him to the ER hoping it was just a false alarm, but he was hospitalized yet again, this time back into St. David's ICU. His white blood cell count was 16,900; other tests pointed again to bacterial infection from the aortic graft. His doctors at St. David's, now so familiar with his care, changed his IV antibiotics once again and rapidly rehydrated him; then they called Drs. Estrera and Khalil in Houston to inform them of this new development. What would this do to Mark's planned surgery just a week away?

His Houston doctors, after much deliberation, decided that the window of opportunity to get Mark well enough for surgery was simply not presenting itself. That infected aortic graft had to come out to prevent further bouts of sepsis. There would be no waiting for next week. They wanted him transferred by ambulance, tomorrow if he could be stabilized enough.

With just twenty-four hours of vigorous treatment at St. David's, Mark's temperature and labs nearly normalized, raising hope that they could buy some more time. Yet both he and Nancy realized that they couldn't rely on his remaining sepsis-free for much longer. Reluctantly, they agreed with Dr. Estrera about replacing the aortic graft as soon as possible.

The next day, Mark and Nancy were once again strapped into the back of an ambulance headed for Houston. The weather was now even more cold and damp than when they recently had made the same miserable trip. The pictures taken before closing the ambulance doors showed Mark smiling, always positive. But that smile didn't last long.

• • •

CHAPTER 29

DECEMBER 10, 2013

NOT LONG INTO THE TRIP, Mark told Nancy and the attendant that he didn't feel well; later, he said he felt terrible. Because of traffic, the cold bumpy ride lasted five hours. Despite all the efforts to stabilize him during the ride, Mark's attendant had to rush him directly into ICU at Hermann. By the time he reached his room, he was severely short of breath and had a high heart rate.

The initial assessment was that the aorta and its graft had started to leak again; his hemoglobin was dropping precipitously; blood transfusions were begun at once. Labs showed, too, that, despite seeming so much better at St. David's, he was still septic.

I had remained in Austin with the children. Nancy called me around midnight; her voice was fraught with tears and fear, reminiscent of that awful day in September.

"Mom! Something's happened to Mark. He told me he thought he was dying. He said he couldn't breathe. They rushed the crash cart into his room and threw me out. I'm just so afraid."

I was struggling to think like a doctor. I was with the kids in Austin and couldn't leave quickly. I suggested she track down the charge nurse. Maybe go to the main ICU desk and appeal for help. I kept talking, the cell phone an umbilical cord between the two of us.

Eventually, the nurses allowed her back into Mark's room; they had not had to shock him or do CPR, but they told her Mark was now confined to bed. With the aorta leaking, he could handle no stress on his heart. His doctors were poised to put him on the ventilator, but his breathing slowed down and only an oxygen mask was needed at the time. A percutaneous indwelling central catheter (PICC), line was put in to serve as a prolonged IV access; his other veins had collapsed.

Mark's blood cultures grew out Pseudomonas again, so his antibiotic regimen was beefed up once more to fight this most recent bout of sepsis. As his aortic graft leaked, blood was replaced via his PICC line. It was a race against the clock; his surgeons wanted him as healthy as possible for the surgeries that so badly needed to be done, but if that graft went from a leak to a torrent, Mark would die instantly. At the same time, to go to the OR with Mark so unstable, he would be at even higher risk of a bad outcome.

Within three days, Mark's blood cultures normalized; sepsis had been defeated once more, but the leaking graft demanded attention. His hemoglobin had finally risen to 9, thanks to multiple transfusions: 9 grams is a minimum requirement for an aortic surgery, where blood loss could be significant. But clinically he was not nearly as well as when he was discharged from St. David's just a few days prior.

Then his blood pressure began to rise; this was a new problem; medications to lower blood pressure had to be added to take the strain off of his already fragile aorta. It was like walking a tightrope: too high pressure and the aorta and its graft could disintegrate, causing instant death; too low, and the brain would not perfuse properly, causing a stroke. At one point, food formula in the J-tube port had to be stopped because of new abdominal pain. X-rays of the abdomen showed nothing structurally awry—a blessing—and feeding was again begun via vein, or TPN, total parenteral nutrition. Nancy sent home for Mark's favorite small pillow or "Pillow Junior" with a bright new Star Wars pillowcase.

During the next few days, Mark's surgical team discussed the pros and cons of the upcoming surgeries with Mark and Nancy. My other two children flew in, my son Tom to Houston to be at the hospital, and my daughter Carol returned to Austin to help me there with the kids. Wade joined Nancy, too, and Elaine and Mark's sisters and their families arrived in Houston shortly thereafter. Before school let out for Christmas break, Marshall contracted influenza type B, despite having had his flu vaccine. His pediatrician treated him, and Mark's surgeons okayed an ICU visit a few days later, given the time frame, with the stipulation that Marshall be gowned, gloved and masked while around Mark.

Mark's blood pressure issues, blood loss, and recurring Pseudomonas pushed the surgery date out to December 16. Mark was again smiling and positive as usual before heading to the OR. This surgery would be almost a preliminary one: putting the new graft in, but leaving the old one in place until success was assured. Three days later a second, more complicated surgery would remove the old graft, transferring blood flow to the new graft. Then, during the same surgery, attention would be turned to the esophagus and how best to repair and reconnect it.

According to the operative report on that date, Mark's breastbone was once again sawed in half lengthwise, serving as the entryway into his chest. Old wires that had been put in five months ago were removed, and the breastbone had to be reconstructed afterward with stainless steel wire and plastic zip ties. Mark's ascending aorta, the upper part of the huge artery coming from the left heart, was rotated from its normal position in the left upper chest, to behind and to the right of the heart. There it was attached onto a much lower part of the aorta, aptly named the descending thoracic aorta. This rerouting achieved "...a distal ascending-to-descending thoracic aortic bypass." The old graft remained and would be removed during the next surgery. The placement of the new graft was considered a success, and he was sent back to the Cardiovascular ICU in stable condition.

Dr. Estrera was pleased: he told Nancy that everything went well and the next surgery was definitely a *go*. He cautioned, however, that the next surgery was much more complicated and could take up to six or more hours. The best news was that Mark was so stable that he was taken off the ventilator later in the day. Pain and the potential for bleeding were the biggest problems now.

The next two days brought no bad news; Mark continued to recover well; labs were good, and his right lung and his heart were performing normally. Dr. Estrera went over the plan again for Nancy, Mark, and family at Mark's bedside. Dr. Estrera planned to reroute the blood to the newly-grafted bypass he had previously put in, then remove the old graft. This was a longer but necessary route to avoid aortic blood flowing through the oft-infected left chest. Finally, after the clean and freshly-grafted aorta was working well in its new position on the right, the plan was to clean out the left chest cavity once again and remove any damaged esophagus and any remaining fistulous tissue.

Mark would then be on the ventilator for a few days afterward. The doctor expected recovery would be at least several weeks in ICU; then, Mark would be sent to IMCU. From there, he would go back to Austin to heal for several weeks or so and finally come back to Houston to reconstruct the esophagus which would free him from the dreaded spit fistula and its ostomy bag. At this point, all data was optimistic for the surgery scheduled for the next day, around 8:00 a.m. Nancy noted the irony of December 16 and 19 being Mark's dates of surgery: the same dates as in September. She hoped he would continue his streak of good surgical recoveries on those two dates. She both craved and dreaded eight o'clock a.m. to arrive.

CHAPTER 30

• • •

SURGERY WAS DELAYED UNTIL 10:00 a.m. At 1:42 p.m., word was sent to the waiting room that Mark was stable and doing well. At 2:38 p.m., the message was Mark was still doing well. At 4:42 p.m.: Mark was still holding his own. Finally, at 7:15 p.m., Mark came out of surgery. Dr. Estrera sat down with Nancy and the rest of the family for a long discussion.

He spoke of many things but praised Mark's previous surgeons. He noted that Mark's surgery was one of the most difficult he had done in the last several months. First, Mark had developed a severe coagulopathy or blood clotting abnormality, not unusual in severely ill patients. Patients with this condition bleed heavily. Treatment requires multiple transfusions of blood products and addressing the inciting incident, which in this case was the recurring serious infection from the old graft. Mark's blood requirements were massive; during the surgery he had received eleven units of packed red blood cells, three units of Cell Saver, four units of plasma, ten units of cryoprecipitate, and twelve units of platelets: enough to fill up several healthy people.

The most difficult and most important part of Dr. Estrera's part of the surgery was to perform what he had intended, but not hurt anything in the process. Because Mark's left lung had been removed in July, the right lung had expanded beyond its usual dimensions, blocking the area where Dr. Estrera needed to work. He told Nancy he had had to remove parts of Mark's fifth and sixth left ribs in order to see adequately inside.

Further, scarring from previous surgeries and infection had made an impenetrable solidified mess of Mark's tissues. Dr. Estrera dictated in his operative report, "…literal carving out of the graft was required using a scalpel blade." This is significant.

In medical school, we were taught the mantra: the scalpel is meant only for opening the skin. Having to resort to using a scalpel inside the patient is testimony to the tremendous difficulty this surgical field presented. Dr. Estrera said he had to chip away, literally, at the old graft for two hours. This meant that scar tissues from Mark's three previous chest surgeries were again impenetrable. I recalled how Dr. Kesler had used the words "labor-intensive" to describe his own surgical journey through Mark's adhesions last July. Now it had been Dr. Estrera's turn, and it was just as difficult, if not more so.

He also told us that he had had to use the heart/lung machine because all the carving made safe clamping of the aorta impossible. Clamping is essential in simple aortic cases; without it, the blood would simply pour into the surgical field.

But Mark's case was not simple, so the alternative, deep hypothermic circulatory arrest, was necessary. In this procedure, the patient's body is cooled down; the patient responds similarly to a bear hibernating: temperature, heart rate, metabolic rate, and respirations slow. The heart/lung machine actually takes over circulation and oxygenation while the patient's body remains in a sort of suspended animation, allowing the surgeon to do his repair.

Mark was in circulatory arrest for sixteen minutes, not an extreme amount of time. His lowest temperature was 18.3 degrees Celsius, equivalent to 64.9 degrees Fahrenheit. Everything went well, the old graft was out, the new graft was working, there was no sign of any infection, and packings were put in, to be taken out the next day.

Wait a minute! The next day? What about the esophagus? Wasn't that to be addressed today too? Dr. Estrera clarified: there had simply not been enough time to spend on the esophagus as had been planned, so a return to the OR the next day to remove packings and check the esophagus was needed. A wound VAC was also used; this applies suction to the incision to help it drain. Because of all these issues, Mark was, of course, still intubated and on the ventilator, now listed in critical condition.

Nancy and the family were familiar with the scar-tissue difficulties Dr. Estrera described, but he referred to it as "all pretty straightforward." And, he added, he had good news. He had looked quickly at the esophagus and felt it was in better shape than expected. Less of it had rotted than had been thought three months ago. Although he deferred to Dr. Khalil, the thoracic surgeon who would address the esophagus the next day, he noted that it might even be possible to salvage and just support the distal or bottom end of the esophagus. He added that it would be a huge benefit not to have to remove and reconstruct the esophagus from some other body tissue like the intestine. Everyone smiled; maybe this would be a merry Christmas after all!

Mark was then returned to his room in CVICU, and after a while, Nancy went to the cafeteria to grab a bite to eat. Coming back, turning the last corner in the CVICU hallway, she froze: why were all those serious-faced nurses hurrying into and out of Mark's room?

CHAPTER 31

• • •

NANCY GRAPPLED WITH THE SCENE before her; when she had left just a short while ago, she had dared to be happy. Yes, Mark was in critical condition, but things had gone well despite difficulties; what was this all about?

Dr. Estrera stepped out of Mark's room and pulled Nancy aside; in the short time since they had talked, Mark had had a stroke. He was now paralyzed on his right side and couldn't speak beyond grunting. Nancy was devastated by good news being replaced so quickly by such enormously bad news; she struggled to make sense of it.

Dr. Estrera told her there was no bleed in the brain. This was of course good news; no bleeding meant no need to stop it. A later CT scan noted no clot, either. No clot meant nothing to remove. Mark's was considered a low-oxygenation or anoxic stroke, which is less of a threat than a clot or bleed.

Dr. Estrera stressed that since Mark was young, he should be able to survive the stroke and improve. He told Nancy it was a reversible situation but a slow one. Getting through this would take all of Mark's patience and strength. He told her he was concerned, but not so much as to postpone the remaining surgery. He finished by saying that he was happy with the nurses that night; they had worked tirelessly to keep Mark's condition from worsening. Later that evening, Dr. Estrera told Nancy that he had even noted a little bit of progress on Mark's right side. Still, this was devastating news, a setback that would complicate everything.

The next morning, Mark was returned to the OR. Dr. Estrera removed the packing from the day before. He noted no active arterial bleeding, but the coagulopathy, or bleeding abnormality, remained. The good news was that both the far and near ends of the new aortic graft were not bleeding. The many raw surfaces, from all the extensive chiseling and carving were oozing, but this was not unexpected.

Then Dr. Khalil took over to address the esophagus. He found healthy esophageal tissue, but when he tried to form a watertight seal of the esophageal wall, only the first two sutures held, due to the inner lining of the esophagus being "completely frozen by scar tissue."

More scar tissue to deal with: Dr. Khalil now had his turn, just as Dr. Kesler and Dr. Estrera had had theirs before him. Thus, the hopes of viability of the esophagus were, upon his further examination, found to be false. A chest muscle, the serratus anterior, was brought around to make that watertight seal, bringing both a blood supply and muscular bulk to allow it to heal. Mark's chest was again irrigated, packed and covered again with a wound VAC. He had been in the OR for two hours, returning to the CVICU still on life support and in stable but critical condition. The third and final surgery was to be Tuesday, December 24.

Later that evening, Mark ran a fever of 101.5. Cultures were done, checking for infection. His heart rate went up to 130. Otherwise, he was moving his left side but not the right. He was, however, able to track a bit better with his eyes.

The next day brought some good news from Dr. Estrera; Mark had no new issues to address. His blood pressure was coming up well; in fact, while in the OR the day before, Dr. Estrera had run his pressure up high to check the sutures; his heart did fine, and there was no bleeding.

Later that day, Mark's cultures again showed evidence of infection for Pseudomonas; now, however, Streptococcus had also grown out again, too. A stronger IV antibiotic cocktail was begun. His heart rate came down to the 90s and his temperature normalized at 99. Blood pressure remained stable at the higher level. Mark even began to nod his head past the midline of his body: a first! Nancy put a picture of Tabor and Marshall with Santa in Mark's left hand, and he manipulated it normally.

Two days after Mark's second surgery, Dr. Estrera returned Mark to the OR intending to clean out the chest cavity, and allow Dr. Khalil to reposition the serratus anterior muscle and remove more ribs. Instead, he chose only to irrigate the chest cavity and reapply the wound VAC, giving Mark more time to remain on the ventilator, rest, and heal. Mark's brain was injured in the stroke, and he felt a bit of waiting would be a good idea before entering the OR for yet another surgery. Mark was returned to the ICU, this time in stable condition.

"What about further brain injury at these surgeries?" Nancy asked. Dr. Estrera assured her this was not a danger as before; the chest cavity surgeries to come were not vascular, and the risk was thus not an issue as before. All the work done on the aortic bypass graft was functioning well. Dr. Estrera reassured Nancy, "His plumbing is working just fine."

It was now December 23; although still on the ventilator, Mark's eyes lit up when a loved one came into his line of sight. Pain medication was reduced to see how he would respond. When his neurologist pinched his right foot, he grimaced: a good sign. Cardiac and blood pressure medicines were discontinued. Just IV fluids, antibiotics and less pain medicine remained. Diuretics were added short term to reduce expected fluid build-up from tissues after surgery. All in all, he seemed to be progressing, especially with the major aortic surgery being deemed a success.

Dr. Khalil came later in the day to have a long talk with Nancy and Wade. As Mark's thoracic surgeon dealing with the esophagus, his first task was to ensure that the left chest cavity would never become infected again. He explained how he intended to remove even more back ribs and essentially collapse the posterior chest wall, attaching it close to the back of the heart. This maneuver would minimize the area of that cavity, decreasing the risk of reinfection.

Another option was to do nothing: but this meant, basically, for the rest of Mark's life, waiting for and wondering if, infection might once again be on the horizon. If that were the decision, Dr. Khalil would need to convert the neck ostomy to a permanent one in his chest and run the risk of that getting infected, too.

He further told them that he had been in practice for nearly fifty years, had seen so much, and thought it was bordering on a miracle that Mark's body had survived all this trauma. Recovering from the last surgery in the morning would be a major undertaking as well. He used the word "brutal" to describe what he planned to do in the OR.

The stroke presented the biggest setback to Mark's overall long-term healing, though; paralysis of his right arm and leg would constitute a huge barrier to rehabilitation of his painful left chest. How could he perform physical therapy when two of his major chest-supporting ribs had just been removed, with four more planned to be removed tomorrow? When his left chest cavity would have just been surgically crushed in? When he didn't have a left lung? When his breast bone had just been re-opened and closed with steel wire and zip-ties? When his only consistent communication was the word *"Ow?"* When just moving about would cause pain for months? How was any of that going to work?

All this was difficult to discuss and to consider the alternatives, none of which were without risk and pain. Dr. Khalil assured them that they could sleep on it, ask more questions in the morning, or even change their minds. He finished by telling Nancy and Wade that Mark would be in the hospital for at least several more weeks; after that, he'd need extensive rehab before going home. He said he felt Mark's determination would translate into lots of progress with that rehab. Reconnecting the esophagus would be "way down the road." Removal of the dreaded neck ostomy bag and reconstruction of the esophagus, Mark's biggest complaint since September, would again, just have to wait.

Nancy and Wade discussed it and prayed into the wee hours for God's guidance to help Mark make the right decision about moving ahead for this fifth trip to the OR in eight days. Elaine had brought some blessed water from Lourdes; Mark agreed to being anointed with it, signifying his choice to go ahead with surgery. Once his decision was made, they supported it.

But now Nancy had one more problem to deal with: tomorrow was Christmas Eve. She had hoped to be able to drive home to Austin, but now that was simply out of the question. What if Mark died in surgery? She wanted to be with him. But Tabor and Marshall were so young; how could she deprive them of having at least one parent there for Christmas Eve?

Over a year later, she told me how she had reached her decision that night. Taking a break, she had gone alone to the hospital chapel to pray for guidance. There, a Bible lay open, and as she read, she realized this was a passage she and Mark had chosen to be read at their wedding.

"At last, I knew what I had to do." She stayed.

She FaceTimed me back in Austin to tell her final decision. Her face was haggard and ravaged with stress, tears streaming down her cheeks. Her voice was hoarse from crying.

"I don't want the kids to see me like this; I'm just going to call them and try to explain what's going on." Hoping to share at least a semblance of normalcy for Tabor and Marshall, Nancy called. Instead of understanding, they were irritable and angry that they again were separated from Nancy and Mark, stuck at home with me, their Nana. Instead of Christmas cheer, only fear and loneliness resounded at both ends of the cell phone. Putting them to bed that night was painful for both the children and me. My mantra, when surrogate-parenting Tabor and Marshall, was simple, "Lord, help me say what I should and not say what I shouldn't." Far too often, I fell short of the mark.

Christmas Eve finally arrived. My son Tom later told me that Mark's face, for the first time, showed fear as they wheeled him out of CVICU toward the OR.

This surgery lasted nearly three hours. Dr. Khalil noted the serratus anterior muscular flap to the esophagus looked healthy. There was no active bleeding. He removed the back portions of a total of six left ribs. This left essentially a floppy slab of chest wall in the back, and this slab was collapsed all the way to the back side of the heart. This was to minimize the left chest cavity and eliminate as much space as possible to prevent further infection. Potent antibiotics and painkillers in solution were used as a final rinse in what was left of the cavity, and Mark's incision was closed completely.

Mark's coagulopathy or bleeding difficulty had been improving as he healed and fought the Strep and Pseudomonas infections. His bone marrow had finally kicked in to produce new blood cells. This time he had needed only four units of packed red blood cells and two units of fresh frozen plasma.

Nancy was told that the next forty-eight hours would be critical; bleeding and infection were two enemies to watch out for. Dr. Khalil said Mark would need at least seven to ten more days in CVICU. He was going to be taken off the ventilator in a few hours after surgery if all went well. When he was stable, they could discuss where he should go for rehab; at that point, the decision seemed light-years away.

That night was a difficult one for Mark. He was in great pain; when he was given painkillers, his blood pressure dropped. His heart started to race again. The ventilator irritated him; he was agitated. Doctor Khalil felt he needed to remain on the ventilator overnight; he could be extubated the next day if he remained clinically stable.

Christmas morning arrived; Mark passed his breathing test and could come off life support. What a Christmas gift! One of several chest tubes was to come out later in the day, as well as an arterial line from his lower arm and a central line from his neck. He was given a bath and made more comfortable. A special bed to prevent skin breakdown was ordered. Dr. Khalil noted that everything looked very good: no excessive bleeding, no fever, and no infectious signs.

Still, there was only minimal movement on Mark's right side, and his only clear word was "Ow" when he felt pain, which was almost constantly. He was communicating, though, and in fairly good spirits.

I had stayed in Austin with the kids, of course, with much help from other Clifton family members and friends. They had wrapped presents, taken the kids to see Santa, taken them to movies, baked holiday cookies with them, and generally filled the gaps that the lack of Nancy and Mark made so painful this time of year. Elaine had the traditional Christmas

Eve gift opening and dinner at their home in Austin; I took Tabor and Marshall, and they were glad to go; yet the mood was decidedly quieter, less boisterous.

Tabor, Marshall, and I set out for Hermann Hospital in Houston after presents under the tree were unwrapped and pictures had been taken. The kids didn't have their usual Christmas glee. The weather was cold and rainy. There just wasn't much to be merry about.

At Hermann, gowned and gloved, we all got to visit Mark for a very short time. He looked fragile and broken; yet, after all his body-changing surgeries and a big stroke, he was alive and 'there.' He was not very responsive, but it was obvious that the kids were the apple of his eye. As Nancy said, "Thank you, Baby Jesus."

She later texted a thread to the family, "Mark moved his head to the right!!! First time."

When visiting hours were over, the kids and I left for a familiar-named motel where I had reserved a room. It was now dark, after 9 p.m. on Christmas Day; we were all worn out after the emotional events of the day. Off I drove in Nancy's van with visions of a warm and comfortable room dancing in my head. I looked forward to treating both the kids and me to room service for bedtime ice cream. But that motel was nowhere to be found.

CHAPTER 32

. . .

THE STREETS WERE EMPTY, STORES were closed, and my GPS was leading me in circles. Finally, there was that familiar-named motel, squashed back behind a rusting chain link fence under a highway overpass. This was it? The sign confirmed that it was.

I was so miserable that despite my misgivings, I checked in. It was essentially deserted except for an attendant. The kids by that time had caught a second wind and thought the place was grand. They didn't notice the grimy empty concrete pool outside our window. Uncomfortable, I called to request a different room and was told they were remodeling, and no other room was available.

I was paralyzed with exhaustion and fear, unconvinced that we were safe. I called John, who got us a room at a Hilton within walking distance from Hermann. Then I called the front desk to check out. The kids were reluctant to leave, but when they saw my face, they complied.

I stopped at the checkout desk; the attendant gallantly tried to change my mind, reminding me I had already paid for three days. At that point I could only say I just didn't feel safe with two young children in tow. As we wheeled out our luggage, the front desk man was apologetic; I told him I understood, but I felt I had to go. As I was closing the rear door of the van, the attendant came running out.

"There will be no charge. Merry Christmas." Grateful, I hugged him quickly; then we pulled out onto a rainy freeway.

Thanks to John, when we reached the Hilton, the staff was waiting for us; the hotel was also nearly empty at Christmas. But here we were at peace, feeling almost adopted by the staff, who showered us with attention. The kids quickly learned the wait staff's name since the person who brought ice cream before bedtime that night was the same one who served us dinner in the restaurant the following night. We had even been upgraded to a suite; we felt we were cocooned in the lap of luxury. We were safe and close by Hermann Memorial.

The rest of our stay in Houston was spent visiting Mark. Since we could walk to Hermann, we got in a bit of exercise. Nearby Rice University and Hermann Park made it easy to get outdoors between visits. In the park the kids ran about; one day we were waiting for the miniature train to take us around the park; Marshall stared at a young boy on his dad's shoulders; I heard him say, to no one in particular, "My dad will never be able to do that ever again." It broke my heart. He was right.

From then until New Year's Day, Mark continued to progress. His chest tube was shortened, he passed a swallowing test so he could eat. His incisions began to heal. Nancy wrote in CaringBridge on December 31, 2013, "Despite pain, discomfort, agitation, lack of control, feelings of loss, Mark perseveres."

The agenda at Hermann, now, was simply healing. Multiple doctors made daily rounds with similar reports: just give him time to heal up from those five trips to the OR in eight days, plus a major stroke. Both Dr. Estrera and Dr. Khalil assured us that Mark was doing well so far and that vital signs were solid. Mark's ID doctor felt his infection was finally coming under control.

Nancy began discussions with them concerning where best to send Mark after discharge from the hospital. He would be in ICU for at least a few more days, then sent to intermediate care, and then possibly to a long term acute care (LTAC).

This process sent a chill along Nancy's spine. She recalled Mark's poor outcome at the SNF in Austin; she wanted nowhere like that. It made perfect sense to her that he was now in much worse shape than he had been when he was discharged from Round Rock back in October; she wanted a stroke rehabilitation hospital. There was discussion of Hermann's nearby sister institution, TIRR Memorial Hermann, right down the street. TIRR stands for Texas Institute of Rehabilitation and Research. It had successfully treated some difficult cases for high-powered patients, names Nancy recognized from national news reports. It seemed like a logical choice.

Mark was encouraged to cough to keep his remaining lung clear, but this was excruciating, having had six partial ribs removed and his breast-bone cracked open. Pain medicines seemed inadequate, yet he had to be clear enough to cooperate with instructions. He was also unable to calm himself; he struggled to communicate; his stroke had caused expressive aphasia: he knew what he wanted to say but it came out in nonsense syllables. Apraxia was another issue. This means that he had trouble making his mouth and tongue enunciate correctly. "Don't know," come out as "No, no." He knew what his cell phone was, and that he wanted it, but could not figure out how to use it. All this lack of control was extra maddening to him because he is right handed, and his right arm and leg were paralyzed. At one point early on, Nancy was able to translate his response to his neurologist, who requested Mark to squeeze his hand; Mark mumbled what sounded like, "I don't want to." This was considered a major success.

Mark also got confused; tests were run to see why. There was always the fear of going back on the ventilator if his oxygen became too low; fortunately, that was never an issue. His oxygen saturations were at 99 to 100 percent, spectacular for just one lung.

Overall the message from all his caregivers was keeping Mark focused on healing; we were encouraged to talk to him, read to him, and show him family photos and work with the therapists who came daily. He needed familiar voices, familiar touches, and familiar music. Nancy brought in his favorite relaxing CD's, his cell phone, and the last calendar he had made in 2012.

In the next few days, there were tiny celebrations. When told his sisters were on the way, Mark responded, eyebrows lifted, what sounded like "Really?"

When told the kids were coming, he looked sad and said what passed for, "I really, really, really miss them." He, at that point, could not recall their recent daily visits.

It was now the first week of the new year and on January 4, Mark sat on the side of his bed for the first time. He was allowed to sit in a wheelchair so he could be wheeled to a window to see the sky. The next day, his blood pressure, oxygen and heart monitors were removed. His bloodwork normalized. He would have to remain on antibiotics for an entire month, nonstop. Nancy shaved Mark's face, leaving him a spiffy 1970's type mustache; she sent it around by cell phone.

Dr. Estrera was pleased with Mark's healing. He felt it best not to rush to a rehab facility just yet, but to continue considering the alternatives: Austin or Houston? Nancy felt that despite the convenience of Mark being back in Austin, she was afraid that the two-hour trip back to Houston in case of emergency was just too much to gamble with. The more she considered TIRR, the more she felt that was the right answer, despite being away from home and the children even longer.

Dr. Estrera assured her that TIRR had a national reputation as one of the nation's best brain rehab facilities; TIRR, pronounced "tier," had a long history of being recognized for its quality care. A bonus was that Mark's infectious disease doctor made rounds there too and could follow Mark's continued recovery.

Nancy decided, after much thought, that with all his other issues, the proximity to Hermann, and continuity of care, TIRR was the best choice. But how long would Mark be there, she wondered. The answer was not a pleasant one: weeks to months.

Now she had to repeat her tough decision-making from Christmas: go home with the kids or stay with Mark? If both, what kind of schedule? Who would stay with the kids in her absence and get them to school and all their activities? If she stayed in Houston that long, where would she sleep? Do laundry? Eat? This was not going to be easy in any aspect. Everyone in the family assured her of the same thing: we'll take care of the kids and Austin issues; you stay there for Mark. We'll figure out the details as we go along.

On January 11, a month after admission to Hermann, Mark was cleared for transfer to TIRR. He was able to sit up for three entire hours and wore clothes and shoes for the first time since arriving. Life was looking up! He was "getting out" of Hermann Hospital! Social Services had done their job well, and the transfer was ready to go. Getting into TIRR, however, was a problem.

• • •

CHAPTER 33

JANUARY 2014

NANCY, MARK'S DOCTORS, AND SOCIAL Services had agreed that Mark's highly complex medical case required a private room. Mark's emotional state at that point was still very fragile. At Hermann, when Nancy walked around to the other side of the curtain in his hospital room, he became frantic, wondering where she was. His only clearly-understood utterance was still "Ow," meaning pain. He needed extra care due to his stroke and all his surgeries, feeding tube and ports, ostomy, chest tube, and now, as a result of the long-term antibiotics, frequent diarrhea. He was on strict "sternal precautions,' meaning he could not put any body weight on his hands or arms; this made moving and sitting, even in bed, particularly difficult.

At the last minute before transfer to TIRR, Nancy was told there were no private beds available. Mark could, however, stay in a room with another man until a single room became available. Feeling she had no choice, she reluctantly agreed. Feeling he needed a 24/7 advocate, Nancy also wanted a family member always at his side.

Off he went by ambulance to TIRR, where he met his roommate, George (not his real name), recovering from a motorcycle accident. George's brain injury had affected him by making him shout and curse loudly at all times of the day and night.

Kellye, Mark's sister, spent the first night at TIRR with Mark so Nancy could sleep in a real bed at her dad's home in Houston; she had been sleeping in a chair in Mark's room. Kellye soon made it clear to the staff that Mark was not in a good place. George's behavior frightened Mark to the point that Mark had to be restrained by tying him in the bed. It took a long few days, but finally Mark was placed in a single room.

TIRR is known nation-wide for its successes with brain-injured patients, whether from stroke or trauma. Many patients were older outpatients, but most inpatients were healthy, less than thirty years-old, and victims of trauma—motorcycle injuries.

Mark was none of these. He was forty-one, but he had been very ill for six months; he had no use of his right arm and leg and was unable to speak except in monosyllables. He was unable to get out of bed, go to the bathroom, or even eat or brush his teeth without help. He had to learn how to do everything left-handed. Nor was he himself psychologically; he was in constant pain from the recent surgeries; he also had the chest tube, feeding tube, and esophageal ostomy to deal with. At that point, it was impossible to gauge much about his thought processing or intelligence level. We were just glad for the rudimentary Mark we could witness from time to time.

It was often that I looked at Mark and grieved about the huge height from which he had fallen. Here was the brainchild, the go-to Dell computer wizard, one of the few who understood how this new Cloud concept worked and who was heading up Dell to help move it forward. Here was the vivacious camera-wielding clown on the Maine beach, making us laugh with his antics. Here was the proud father of two miracle children he thought he'd never have; the proud husband of my daughter; the goofy son-in-law running down the street after his beloved runaway dog. Here was the Mark grown men had sobbed about when it looked like he would die. Here was an Olympic torch of a man, now reduced to a mere flicker. My heart ached for him and his family.

He was broken in so many ways; how could he possibly be the same after so much? How could his brain handle all the computer complexities he used to take for granted? Who was he, and what made him keep going? Would he be able to catch up after so much time off? What if he gave up? The implications of all these thoughts weighed heavily on my mind. What would eventually happen to these four Cliftons I loved so much?

I purposely did not share these thoughts with any of them. Nancy and Mark both, all along, insisted that Mark would go back to work as soon as he slogged through all this. Nancy made it clear that there would be no other outcome, no matter how awful it was at the time. Mark, less verbal due to the stroke, remained forceful when he stated on many occasions, after some weeks at TIRR, "I want to be happy and skillful," or "I want to be happy and productive."

One cold morning in late January, Mark's speech therapist asked that I step out for a while; I went to the TIRR cafeteria, sipped coffee and filled prescriptions electronically for my medical practice back in Dallas. I realized that I had been functioning for months as a sort of long-distance doctor, rarely being in the office and doing much by email and telephone. I was already in my late sixties and had talked about retiring in the next few years. The thought bubbled up, *why wait?* I had been in private solo family practice for twenty-four years. I was tired; my family needed me, and that's where I really wanted to be. With the help of many people from Methodist Hospital System in Dallas, my CPA, and my attorney, I would go on to retire in April of that year.

At night Mark had to have splints on his right leg and arm to prevent contractures. He had to wear a compressive glove on his right hand to prevent swelling. Getting it on to his flaccid right hand was next to impossible, even for his caregivers. Still at only 142 pounds, he was all bones. He couldn't fit into a regular wheelchair: one of his doctors, looking at Mark's long legs crammed into a regular wheelchair, exclaimed, "You have the longest femurs I've ever seen." I teased Mark in the wheelchair, saying he looked like he was riding a tricycle.

Being on a cocktail of antibiotics for months continued the frequent diarrhea, and he was appalled to have to wear diapers; we soon learned to call them "briefs" as the aides referred to them.

The daily routine was not easy or comfortable, but we all learned to adjust to it, Mark having the toughest job of all. A typewritten personal schedule was taped to his door every day, at about 6:00 a.m. I dreaded to hear them attach it, since that meant another exhausting day was beginning. By six-thirty, the aides would get him out of bed, clean him up, remove his splints, dress him, and help him with medications and breakfast (both tube and oral feedings) so the therapists could come get him around seven o'clock.

It was much like being in college again; there was, however, no way to cut class, nor did he try to, no matter how bad Mark felt. His therapies were numerous: physical, occupational, speech, and music, among others. There were rest periods between classes at times, so he could be wheeled back to his room, but merely getting him in and out of his wheelchair and keeping him clean ate up much of his rest time. Therapy sessions were one-on-one and took at least five hours daily; at times, they lasted eight hours. A washer and dryer on the wing allowed Nancy to do laundry. She snacked and grabbed a few meals from the cafeteria. She slept on a fold-out chair in his room, living out of a suitcase.

There were times I could hardly stand to watch as Mark struggled to re-learn to walk. He was tethered to a harness which ran in a track around the ceiling of the gym. The official name was the Vector, but it struck fear in any who had to rely on it. We nicknamed it Lector after the merciless movie character. It was adjusted by straps to fit the patient like a toddler in a baby swing. But the patient's legs had to touch the ground to send the neurological message to the brain that legs were meant for walking. In stroke patients like Mark, his right leg had forgotten what that felt like. He had no use of his right arm, either, so it had to be immobilized in a special sling; otherwise, it flopped like a broken wing and got in his way. As he was suspended in the body harness, he had a therapist on both sides. Tiny Rita beside him would scoot his unresponsive right leg along; he was simply unable to move it by himself. All the while, his body reeled from the pain of trying to remain upright after all those recent brutal chest surgeries.

With his right side paralyzed and his left chest cavity hurting from surgery, trying to walk and balance were excruciating and painstaking. At times, I wanted to stop the therapists; his agony was so obvious; yet their demand for "one more minute" continued, and he kept on trying. When we'd get back to his room to recuperate and get ready for the next session, he'd often drop into an immediate deep sleep. And then, sometimes as soon as thirty minutes later, he'd get up and do it all again.

Mark relearned some of his swearwords, using them both for pain and frustration; Nancy said she was sure everyone could hear him while he was in a session in the echoey gym. He was often enraged by not being able to put his thoughts into words, so he just swore instead.

This, of course, was not the authentic Mark we all knew and loved. It took a while, but the nurses and aides came to understand Mark's underlying kind and sweet disposition despite his inability to express himself. They enjoyed his sense of humor and several went out of their way to pamper him. Pam, his favorite aide, would do him extra little favors, like an extra shower after an unusually tough and sweaty day. Other staff liked to "give him a hard time" when really, they were encouraging him, and he was aware of that and reacted well.

There were a few precious humorous moments. TIRR trained all of us how to help Mark, since we would be his primary caregivers back home. The therapist showed me how to maneuver to get Mark both into and out of his wheelchair. It took a lot of practice since we were nearly equal in weight but he towered almost a foot over me in height. When I thought I had the transfer drill down, I tried it on my own one day; but I kept failing, unable to get him out of the chair and into bed. Finally, looking me straight in the eyes, Mark used his functional left hand, reached down, and unfastened the seat belt.

By January 21, Mark's PICC line and IV antibiotics were discontinued. With antibiotics gone, mercifully, the diarrhea resolved. In the gym with the help of the Vector, he walked fifteen feet. This caused cramps in his right leg as the muscles relearned the mechanics of walking. A week later, his ID doctor pronounced him infection-free. Sternal restrictions were released. A few days later, he stood up by his bed for the first time. Mark worked himself to the point of exhaustion. He was beginning to speak a little more, a little clearer; staff could now better understand him.

There were the usual ups and downs with his J-tube port. Eventually he was well enough to use the G or gastric port of the GJ-tube. This translated to relative freedom from clogging, since the G port was larger.

Nancy started to take two- or three- days' sabbaticals in Austin to see the kids and look for a facility Mark could transition to, upon release from TIRR. A family member was always at his bedside since he still was not completely himself mentally and emotionally. Loud noises would startle him and cause him to cry out in alarm. At times of frustration he would shake the left rail of his bed as a prisoner would his shackles.

But Mark progressed. His weight creeped up higher in the 140s, medications were decreased, and he was able to handle bolus tube feedings instead of the continuous pump; this gave him a certain degree of freedom, not to have to drag the pump around or be forced to listen to it.

Nancy had long discussions with his therapists and doctors about whether Mark should be discharged to the Grapevine home or an Austin facility. On her short trips home, she visited several in the Austin area, but none seemed like a good fit. Just thinking about Mark having more freedom and going home to Austin put an unaccustomed but welcome positive spin on life. But on February 3, everything changed.

CHAPTER 34

• • •

THAT MORNING, MARK BEGAN SUDDENLY to shake and stare off to the right, unable to change his gaze. Was this another stroke? A seizure? He was taken back at once by ambulance and readmitted to Hermann ICU. Tests showed only a very low magnesium level but no new brain or heart event. How could that be possible when his intake was totally controlled by the G-port of his tube? It seemed he was losing magnesium somehow, so it was added to his medication regimen. Once his magnesium level was corrected, he quickly normalized. Just twenty-four hours later, he was pronounced well enough to return to TIRR. Of course, there was a glitch; his private room had been given away, but after much haggling, warrior Nancy convinced the social worker of Mark's special needs, and Mark returned to his "home room."

Mark's progress in all areas did improve but slowly, so slowly. He resisted all group therapies, but one-on-one, he did well. His innate intelligence and impish sense of humor at times revealed themselves, allowing his therapists insight into who he really was. For instance, one day his speech therapist left sticky-notes all over his room, identifying objects such as window and bathroom. Each day she would review them with Mark. One day he successfully enunciated the words, "I need to go to..." and then he stopped.

She capitalized on the opportunity that he had articulated so well, jumping in and repeatedly saying, "You have to go where, Mark? Where do you have to go? Go where? Go where?"

Mark was getting irritated with her rapid-fire questioning and finally slowly but quite clearly said, "Go to hell!"

She was totally surprised and a bit taken aback: how do you reward that new comeback? Nancy had a tough time stifling her laughter; this was so like Mark! Another time he was being shown images of objects that he had to name: a ball, a tree, a cup. One picture was what the therapist called a television. Mark corrected her and managed to get out, "That's a desk top computer screen." It was! That time, laughter and high fives abounded.

Tabor and Marshall visited. Mark was listening for them; he heard them as soon as the elevator doors opened. His face beamed and he smiled and shouted, "Kids!"

After Tabor dashed into the room, she played his beloved "The Eyes of Texas are Upon You" on the recorder, bringing tears to his eyes. Marshall drew pictures, giving them to Mark with a hug. At home, the kids had made a Dad-vent calendar, counting down the days until Mark was due home. We had been told that a tentative release date was February 27. Then, about a week later, the date was changed to sometime in March, causing a significant amount of grumbling from Mark.

Nancy decided that Mark would be better off in his real home and not another facility, upon his release from TIRR. Thus, a flurry of activity again overtook the Grapevine Lane home. Nancy's dad procured a real hospital bed; it was set up in the living room; Mark's sisters bought curtains for privacy, and their husbands installed them in tracks they added to the ceiling. They put in grab bars in bathrooms and the master shower. An additional handrail was added to the stairwell to allow Mark to climb both up and down. Wade removed the door to the master bath commode stall. Doorknobs were changed to grab handles. Elaine added further equipment she knew Mark would need.

Mark was now off all narcotics. The final chest tube was removed. There was a question of another infection in the chest cavity but the X-ray looked clear. Mark could say to his sister Kim, "I want to be happy and to use my skills."

Nancy noted on CaringBridge, "Mark refuses to give in to self-pity or doubt."

By March 6, Mark was walking with very little assistance. His right arm, however, did not respond as well to rehab as did his leg. Despite this disappointment, he said to Wade, "I'm so full of fortunate feelings." Mark worked on fiddling with his cell phone: at first he was unable to enter his passcode, but he persisted. Finally, he succeeded, but at that point, his vision was still too uncoordinated to allow him to read or text. He could follow a few favorite television sitcoms again although it frustrated him that he couldn't use the remote to surf, because it was still too confusing.

During Mark's last week at TIRR we family members attended their classes about what to expect at home. Since Mark and Nancy lived in Austin, we couldn't rely on help that was available in Houston, but the information was helpful nonetheless. Therapy was set up at St. David's but this time near downtown Austin, rather than at the familiar and close-by Round Rock facility.

In his final weeks at TIRR, Mark spent time practicing going up and down stairs and was to be allowed one round trip per day at home. He also practiced getting into and out of a car; his aides teased him when, after successfully getting in, he refused to get out. His two occupational therapists gave him a Lego Star Wars set and helped him put it together. Mark was, just before discharge, fitted for a special long-femur, high-back wheelchair for his return home. He would also have the right arm and leg splint and right hand edema glove to use daily.

On March 13, 2014, Nancy drove Mark home in her minivan. Her dad followed. Mark had made great progress in rehab and was infection-free. As the aides lined the hall and wheeled Mark out of TIRR, Mark raised his left hand in a fist and yelled, "Freedom!!" which got a laugh from everyone.

Even more like himself, Mark said, "No more TIRRs (tears)." Everyone laughed at his pun; Nancy was thrilled to hear—here was further proof that Mark was, indeed, on his way back to normal.

The kids had again put out the sign in the yard "Welcome home, Mark" to alert the whole neighborhood that he was coming home at last.

It was an exhilarating but exhausting day for all, especially Mark. The burden of overseeing caregiving rested heavily on Nancy's shoulders. Mark had spent ninety-four awful days in Houston. He was worn out. So was Nancy.

At 5:00 a.m. the next morning, Nancy started preparations for the trip to St. David's for Mark's first therapy session. Getting ready took an hour; getting out of bed, removing some splints and putting on others, dressing, taking vital signs, getting meds and feedings into the G-port of the tube, loading the loaner wheelchair minus its wheels into the back of the van, being sure the go-to-the-hospital bag had everything needed, including more feedings and pain meds; another thirty minutes were spent fighting traffic to get downtown.

In the parking garage, Nancy took out the pieces of the wheelchair and started assembling them. She said with a smile, "This is just like putting the kids' stroller together!" I was amazed at her good humor. Once we rolled Mark inside, we met his team: Bob, a young, boisterous therapist who had no right arm, and Mike, his therapist concentrating on his legs and feet. Speech and vision would come later in the week.

Both Bob and Mike reviewed Mark's long hospital diagnosis chart. They were impressed that he had survived, but they concentrated on what they felt needed to be done. They encouraged him, knowing how difficult and long-term therapy was going to be, trying not to overwhelm him. Bob said to Mark, in summary, "No pressure."

Mark answered, "What's that like?"

They smiled and told him the first lesson was on falling. Bob went first.

"You're gonna fall. It will happen. I'll show you how to get up." He demonstrated for Mark and put him through some scenarios. It was as painful to watch in Austin as it had been back at TIRR. Mark was exhausted, still in pain. But he complied as best he could. Bob's skills, as were Mike's to come, were a comfort to us. Mark was again in good hands.

Mike took over and put Mark through some leg exercise basics. The session was to be four hours, but after two hours, both Bob and

Mike realized that Mark was totally unlike any other patient, and had so many medical issues that he needed to go home early and rest. He was wiped out.

As we left, Bob called out, "Leave the wheelchair in the car from now on; you don't need it."

That night Mark slowly, painfully, climbed the stairs. He refused ever to sleep in the hospital bed again. Once again, that's the way it was. Mark was home.

CHAPTER 35

• • •

SPRING 2014

AND SO IT WENT. EACH day presented new problems, which Nancy attacked head-on. Just five days after coming home, Mark's feeding tube got clogged, requiring yet another trip to Round Rock. Both Nancy and Mark were disappointed; they had been relying on the larger G-tube port solving the clog problem. Although it required a lengthy wait, both Mark and Nancy were once again treated like celebrities. Pictures were taken; the comment of the day was, "You look even better than when you were here last!"

Two weeks after that incident, Mark had chest pain, requiring yet another medical work up; the diagnosis revealed just some pulled chest wall muscles. Mark's' orthotic leg brace, ordered while still at TIRR, arrived; the good news was that it wasn't needed and was sent back. The arm brace Mark had been forced to wear was close to being unnecessary. He would then require just a splint. Biofeedback on his right arm began. When Mark's custom wheelchair, ordered nearly a month before, arrived, it too was sent back. Bob was right—he didn't need it. Mark even had the strength to attend some of Tabor's kickball games, although he had to ride in the loaner wheelchair for the early season games. Later, all he needed was a camping chair with a high back.

Nancy's birthday was April 9. Mark was still having difficulty communicating, but he wanted to get her something special; I called his sister Kim, knowing she would know the perfect gift. And she did: a new jewelry box. Nancy had bought hers before she had even met Mark. When Kim brought the gift to the house, I felt tears in my eyes: engraved on the top were the words, *I want to grow old with you. I love you, Mark.* When it came time for Nancy to open her gift, I slipped out to the deck, but I could hear her crying through the closed door.

A couple of days later, Nancy wrote in CaringBridge, "Mark has surprised us by popping up around the house. He needs very little assistance to get around. It is so unusual to see his 6'3" frame upright again. At first it scared, then delighted us."

Mark was now going to therapy four days a week for four hours at a time. Nancy carried her pre-packed ER visit bag with the usual cans of nutrition, and bundles of all kinds of supplies. At the lunch break, he rested on a therapy table while his "lunch" drained into the G- port in his stomach. He ate "real food" too, which went into the ostomy bag in his left neck. After the infusion and lunch, all the equipment needed to be cleaned, stowed, the ostomy bag emptied and the area cleaned and a bathroom break made. Nancy and other family members drove him the thirty minutes to the hospital for each session, often taking notes and videoing to get "homework." It was massively time-consuming for everyone, but necessary. And it was painful for Mark, but he remained off narcotics, relying on over-the-counter pain relief.

Mark's sense of humor, quick come-backs, and frequent use of puns gradually made their way back into his personality. As his pain level decreased he could find humor much more easily. Nancy described him as goofy and sweet. He was a "regular" at therapy; other patients and all the therapists admired his determination and willingness to try until he was exhausted. On April 29, he moved his right arm up from a dangle position while sitting in a chair: a first! There were tears of joy, applause from both therapists and other patients. Videos were made.

Mark was able to join his family at church. He could now walk slowly in short jaunts through the mall with Nancy and the kids without needing even a walking stick. His memory, both recent and remote, improved. He could stay alone at home with Tabor for short periods of time while Nancy ran errands on the weekends.

Yet there were issues that continued to plague Mark. One was his lack of right-sided vision, consistent with his right arm and leg issues. The medical term is neglect. Despite 20/20 acuity in both eyes, his brain could not interpret the right side of what he saw. Shortly after his stroke in December 2013, he had eaten only from the left side of the plate; both retinas reflected the image properly but his brain could not process it visually. He would bump into familiar furniture; his eyes could see it but his brain could not interpret it. When asked to point to the right, he had to think about it, like someone visualizing where he was on a map. Tabor played a game by spreading different brands of bite-size candies on a tray in front of him. He had to find each one to earn the prize of eating it. One time, for instance, a circuit breaker blew. He went to check the breaker box but couldn't find it on the garage wall. When I went to help, I noticed he was looking just inches to the left of it; his brain couldn't correctly interpret the right visual field signal. His vision therapy homework involved having his left eye patched, forcing his brain to rely more on signals from the right eye. At first, he was unable to put the patch on alone; he had to learn. Driving was out of the question, especially in Austin, rife with bike lanes on the right. This right visual neglect improved but by no means resolved, and by mid-2014, we'd often forget how hard he daily had to struggle with this phenomenon.

Another huge irritation initially was with eating. The right side of his mouth refused to coordinate while chewing, and before he realized it, he would bite the inside of his right cheek with full and painful force, at times yelping in surprise and pain. Mark's right arm and hand use lagged far behind the use of his right leg and foot, adding to his frustration. Unable to perform the simplest movement with his right arm, such as opening a water bottle, would anger him. Eventually he figured out how to do so using his left hand and his teeth. Little by little, though, issues lessened, but the visual right-sided neglect and the right arm paralysis continued to plague him.

Two big events then occurred to uplift the family as Mark continued to improve his walking, coordination, and speech. One was a fundraising golf tournament in his honor, sponsored by a local restaurant, Iron Cactus, on June 5, 2014. Ironically, this was the same venue Nancy had chosen back in 2007 for his cured-of-cancer party. One hundred percent of the proceeds went to Marshall's and Tabor's 529 college savings accounts. Mark spoke his thanks at the celebration; he and Nancy were presented a check for $45,000.00. They both had tears in their eyes as they accepted it. A video of Clifton photos over the years, titled *A FAMILY MAN*, was put together to promote the fundraiser.

The second event was the long-awaited trip to Houston to visit Dr. Khalil, the thoracic surgeon who had worked on Mark's left chest cavity and esophagus in December. Revision and reattachment of the esophagus was the final step to eating normally. Mark was eager to get rid of his feeding tube and ostomy bag. He and Nancy were tired of dealing with the inconvenience and daily hassles.

Off the three of us went to Houston on the morning of June 6, 2014, ready to talk with Dr. Khalil about setting up esophageal reconstruction surgery in a few weeks. First, we visited TIRR where Mark had spent the last three months of his stay in Houston. We had notified Pam, his favorite aide, and she agreed to meet Mark and Nancy there. But when the elevator doors opened and they stepped out into his old unit, they were at first ignored. In just a few seconds, however, Pam and the others rushed to greet them.

"We didn't recognize you! We assumed you'd still be in a wheelchair!" When they realized that this was the man who was so sick and so weak six months ago, they couldn't believe their eyes; some of the nurses cried.

In high spirits after the TIRR visit, we then went to his doctor's appointment. Mark especially was anxious to get this final step over with once and for all. He was a bit surprised when Dr. Khalil's nurse told him that when she had told Dr. Khalil that his next patient was Mark Clifton, Dr. Khalil had said, "That guy is still alive?" We all laughed; that response was so like what we had just experienced at TIRR.

Walking into the exam room, Dr. Khalil wore his "doctor face." Then, staring at Mark a few seconds, his expression morphed into a huge grin. He shook Mark's hand, amazed at how well he looked. He seemed shocked at how this man, whom he had not seen in six months, had transformed from being paralyzed on his right side and only able to say "ow," into a man walking, talking, interacting on a cerebral level. He told Mark how thrilled and proud he was that Mark had done so well, and how he wanted only the best for him.

Then he said, "But…"

CHAPTER 36

• • •

"I HAVE BEEN DOING SURGERY for fifty years, and I have never seen a more complicated case in my life. I can do the surgery we discussed. Reopening you, going in to repair what remains of your esophagus. It may go well, or not well at all.

"In fact, it could kill you. Another option is to do nothing and leave the bag and feeding tube indefinitely. That would be safest, since we would not have a chance to introduce infection again. But if you became infected again, it would be a disaster."

We stared at him like cows in a pasture.

"I have, though," he continued, "a colleague I recommend you see, and her office is right over there," he said, gesturing toward the window.

Nancy was on it, instantly. There was no way Mark would choose to do nothing.

"Who is she? Can we make an appointment today?"

Dr. Khalil's discomfort was visible. He wanted so much to help Mark, but he felt his area of expertise no longer fit Mark's best interest. He explained how this other doctor, Dr. Shanda Blackmon, had concentrated on, among other thoracic areas, esophageal surgery in her relatively young career; she had experience and was into the "latest and greatest," and had even worked on growing esophageal cells in her lab. He and many others held her in high regard. Dr. Khalil had seen her in action and was impressed.

I had, at that moment, enormous respect for Dr. Khalil. As a physician myself, I too had referred patients when I realized another doctor had more experience or expertise than I did in certain areas. Mark had progressed so far beyond what anyone, Dr. Khalil included, had imagined possible. Mark was not the obviously helpless infected stroke victim and debilitated surgery patient he had been in January. This man was more than a survivor; he was actually thriving six months after having had such massive surgical and stroke-related trauma. And so Dr. Khalil bowed to what he thought the best for his patient, and referred Mark to someone else who had earned his respect.

"One thing, though. She has just been recruited to Mayo."

Mark was patiently taking it all in. Nancy, however, was blindsided.

"Mayo? Isn't that in Minnesota? You mean we would have to go all the way to Minnesota for a consultation? Can't she still see Mark here? Couldn't she still do surgery here?"

"She's already gone," Dr. Khalil answered quietly, shaking his head. Nancy was still slack-jawed, thinking of how hard it had been just to navigate life for three months away from home while Mark was in Houston, which was only about 150 miles away from Austin.

"We are not going to Minnesota! Isn't that at least 1,000 miles? Isn't there anyone closer that you could recommend?"

Dr. Khalil understood, but he remained convinced that Dr. Blackmon would be Mark's best bet. He agreed to transfer the records as soon as Dr. Blackmon had an address to send them to.

In the meantime, in the exam room, I did a mental high-five at this change of events. Mayo Clinic: the medical mecca! One of the finest institutions of medicine in America! And they had recruited this Dr. Blackmon; she had to be outstanding. And she had special interest and experience in the esophagus. She sounded hand-picked for us, just the surgeon we needed. I couldn't wait to turn on my cell phone and check her out.

The ride home to Austin was a challenge. Mark said little but seemed willing to do whatever was necessary to get rid of the ostomy bag and feeding tube. In fact, he seemed more exhilarated by the minivan turning over 100,000 miles on the way out of Houston, than by the thought of going to Mayo. Nancy, however, was caught in a vortex of details. *How do we go about finding this doctor? When can she get us in? We are ready now; who knows how long it will take her to see Mark, even if that is possible. When can the surgery be done? What if we don't feel it is a good fit, or if she didn't? What about the kids?* They hadn't had a decent year; everyone in the family was ready to be done with hospitals and doctors and have a little fun. It was June, school was out, they were ready to finish this up, and now this?

I kept quiet except to voice my opinion that this might be a blessing in disguise. Dr. Khalil had done the noble thing: he had deferred to someone he thought could give Mark more of a chance to go on with his now nearly normal life. We'd all just have to figure out how to go about this; first, though, as a doctor familiar with Mark's case, I felt I could be of most help by simply tracking down this wunderkind doctor until Mark and Nancy decided what options there were.

For days, I got online, made phone calls and did research on what other, closer doctors could offer Mark a similar solution to his bag-and-tube-dilemma. There were many options, but all leading to dead ends. Yet, Dr. Blackmon was my real goal; she had, after all, been recommended by someone who had already operated on Mark and who knew her professionally. In my mind, Dr. Blackmon represented a literal answer to all those prayers that had been offered up in such great quantity for Mark.

I gathered data as fast as I could; because I had the magic letters behind my name and had functioned as Mark's family physician a multitude of times, I mercilessly played "the doctor card," finally tracking down Dr. Blackmon on her way to Minnesota. She chatted with me on her cell at the Denver airport. I briefly described Mark's case.

"I know this guy!" she gasped. "I sat next to Anthony Estrera on a plane going to a conference this year. He talked about that impossible case. I'm sure it's the same patient."

"Yep, that's Mark. Can you take him as a patient when you get set up?" She answered by enumerating what all would need to be done; the one word she didn't say was "no." In my opinion, this was divine intervention.

I was amazed at her ability to ask appropriate questions and keep straight the details I told her about Mark, despite never having seen him. Here she stood in an airport, in the process of moving her family from Texas to Minnesota, and trying to squeeze in some hiking before jumping into practice. At the same time, she was actually already on the job putting together a plan for Mark: she would need to gather a surgical team, set up an office, get Mark's records and get him scheduled. Translated: yes, she would accept Mark as a patient.

Thrilled, I spoke to her new administrative Mayo team and put into motion getting Mark's mountains of records to her. Over the next week or so, despite every mix-up and holdup, the details got worked out, Nancy and Mark agreed to see her in Minnesota, and Mark became one of her first patients. Nancy wrote on CaringBridge about the situation. She mentioned also, "This year Father's Day took on special meaning."

In the meantime, Nancy and Mark made another decision.

"We didn't get a chance to have a Clifton vacation last summer; let's see if we can arrange to have the kids go along, and we can all see the polar bears at the Minneapolis/St. Paul Zoo while we're there." The scramble to set up a plan to do just that had officially begun.

Plan? This was more like playing chess with a million pieces on a tight schedule. Just six weeks later found the five of us at Austin-Bergstrom International Airport. First, Mark needed a wheelchair in the terminal. Second, there were no direct flights from Austin to Rochester, and we had to fly through O'Hare in Chicago, doubling all preparations. We would need to take not only the gym bag, but, among a multitude of other things, several days' worth of tube feedings, a wedge pillow to elevate his head, the portable IV pole used to infuse his feedings, all his meds and a pill grinder to pulverize them, extra supplies, his right arm night splint. The airlines informed us we needed a doctor's letter to get the large medical supply suitcase to fly without a charge and to explain why we needed to take these 250 ml paper cans of feedings with us. And, they wanted to know, why were we taking along all these little bottles of water? I wrote the explanatory letter, of course, but it fell to Nancy first to explain this to the airline desk personnel, and then to undergo the necessary TSA interrogations at the gate.

At the gate, Nancy was taken to a special area. Each can of feeding formula had to be scanned, as did each bottle of water. All they had to do with Mark, however, was to see his GJ-tube attached to his abdomen and his ostomy bag adhered to his left neck; no extra scanning was ever deemed necessary for him. The kids and I, each with a carry-on, came through easily too; then all five of us plowed to the gate, regrouping and recounting all the paraphernalia needed for the rest of the trip.

Mark still didn't feel hunger or thirst. Thus, especially in July, Nancy had to give him extra water any time Mark started to sag a bit or complain of exhaustion, which was often. When he felt weak, Nancy attached a large plastic syringe to his G-tube port and slowly poured a bottle of room temperature water into it. She learned how to do this even in the airport or during a flight, and nobody noticed. She also fed him on a schedule by slowly infusing the cans of feedings through the G tube into his stomach. This required filling IV bags with cans of feeding formula, which ran by gravity. He had to receive eight cans daily to ensure enough calories and nutrients. The cans, of course, were not available on any grocery or drug store shelf, so she had to pack enough to last the entire trip. She used the little water bottles to add hydration via his G tube port whenever needed.

The five of us finally arrived in Rochester, Minnesota, and made our way to our hotel in a rental SUV. Nancy set up Mark's medical area with IV pole, medication bottles, pill crusher and fluids; the next morning Nancy and Mark went to Mayo Clinic to meet Dr. Blackmon for the first time.

Dr. Blackmon had clearly done her homework on Mark's case, realizing its complexity and seriousness. She came right to the point. Looking them both in the eye, she said, "We have a problem."

Blindsided again.

• • •

CHAPTER 37

WHILE SIFTING THROUGH MARK'S HUGE chart, Dr. Blackmon had noticed an abnormality in a chest X-ray. It looked like a tiny air pocket. This had been present on previous X-rays and had not changed. Possibly it was just an artifact; before she could go any further, she had to know what this was. This meant, once again, an extra surgery would be necessary before even considering his esophagus, GJ-tube, and ostomy. Now, though, she had to know that Mark was in good enough shape before she entered the left chest cavity to address the air sac, so a laundry list of tests had to be done to prove that he was.

She began by connecting him with several other specialists who made up her new team. He had to see lung specialists, heart specialists, have lab work, breathing tests, CT scans, and an echocardiogram. This would take hours, so I took the kids to the Mall of the Americas, about an hour's drive away. It turned out there were so many tests, Mark and Nancy never did get to see the polar bears, but Tabor, Marshall and I did, while their parents made their way through the huge Mayo system.

Despite Mayo's size, it was a masterpiece of communication and efficiency, with a personal touch. Although the number of tests and new doctors was daunting, Mark and Nancy got everything done on time. They were exhausted in the evening, of course, but we were still able to go out for a meal or take a stroll around a nearby shopping center. Mark and Nancy bought University of Minnesota Goldy Gopher tee-shirts for Tabor and Marshall, of course.

After several days and extensive testing, Mark and Nancy had one final visit with Dr. Blackmon to wrap things up. We had checked out of the hotel, packed the SUV, and were ready to head to the airport after that visit. Then, while I was circling Mayo, Nancy called me on her cell, telling me she and Mark had to stay; one of the scans confirmed there certainly was an air pocket in Mark's left chest cavity. Dr. Blackmon suspected a leak from the stomach. It could be nothing, or it could come back to haunt Mark in the future, starting this whole infectious process all over again. Did the kids want to stay, or go? A quick vote in the backseat confirmed they both wanted to stay; that meant I had to stay, too, while Mark underwent further workup.

This also meant a change of hotels; a conference in Rochester that week had filled the hotels. Hopeful, we returned to our hotel but were told our room was already occupied. We were referred to a sister hotel, where we unpacked in the only two small rooms left. Then came the agony of changing all five flights so we could all go home together after Mark finished with whatever Dr. Blackmon had planned. But at such short notice, all flights were already booked; we faced change fees for flights and the rental car too.

Rental car! In the rush, I had forgotten about it, and now it was late too! I received an email from the company insisting I return it immediately and adding fees to it hourly; I made several phone calls; penalties were reduced, but the extra costs were staggering.

The next two days were consumed with more testing for Mark. Two days later, Mark's results were maddeningly inconclusive. Tabor, Marshall, and I were sent home, but Mark and Nancy had to stay. When I spoke to the airlines yet again, trying to sort out the tickets, I could hear the agent typing on the computer. Then she stopped, taking in a big breath.

"You've had fifteen different tickets on that credit card in the last week!"

All I could manage was a weak, "Yes, I know. Can you help me?"

She could, but it would cost more, and then more, and then even more; all regular seats were already taken, so we had to buy the more expensive ones. We could get out of Rochester, but the connecting cities to Austin were already booked; we could get a better deal in Minneapolis, but the rental car company would charge me even more, since I had rented it originally in Rochester. On and on it went, the dollar signs swirling ever higher.

After Tabor, Marshall, and I left Rochester, Nancy wrote in CaringBridge on July 22, "The air in Mark's chest cavity is not coming from the airway, where Mark's left lung had been removed. It was leaking from the esophagus. The esophagus had bifurcated, or diverged into two pieces, so there were now two branches into the stomach. The new branch was healthy. The old fistulous branch had been patched in Houston in December of 2013, but the patch had failed. There was no leak now, but there may be one in the future."

Dr. Blackmon met with Mark and Nancy yet again to go over all the options. She even offered to do the air-sac surgery the very next day. Since there was no leak now, this was not an emergency. Or, Mark could postpone it, or never do it at all. Mark might go years or even the rest of his life with no further problems. It was impossible to predict what the future held, but it could all fall apart and leak tomorrow or at an unknown time in the future. Then we would be back to September 16, 2013.

What to do? Mark was just not prepared for an unintended surgery tomorrow. This air leak surgery was above and beyond why he had come to Dr. Blackmon in the first place. Even more important to Mark, this surgery would not rid him of the dreaded ostomy bag and GJ-tube. He'd have to come back for that anyhow. With all the adhesions and troubles the other doctors had had in his left chest, he wondered what surprises lay in wait for Dr. Blackmon when she did open him up.

Once again, there were no easy answers. Time away from home over the last week had taken its toll; he missed the kids. He wanted to go home. The thought of another hospitalization with no resolution of the bag and tube was overwhelming. Staying and getting the chest air sac taken care of would be the economical thing to do, but he wasn't even sure he wanted to do it at all. Maybe he could just gamble that it would never come back to haunt him. He was torn. He felt he needed time to churn through all the options and possible outcomes.

He chose to come home to Austin. When they told her, Dr. Blackmon reiterated that when he did come back, it would be only for removing the source of the air pocket. Based on what she found there and what the results were, then the final esophageal reconstruction and resolution of tube and ostomy would be done at a later date. Mark could even come back in a few weeks for the air-pocket surgery, if he so wished. She was most understanding; by that time, they were all much more comfortable together, laughing about both Mark and Dr. Blackmon being University of Texas at Austin graduates. All three of them shared a love of the Longhorns, queso and tacos. She and her husband had three sons, about the same ages of Marshall and Tabor. Nancy and Mark trusted and liked her, but the thought of an additional surgery was impossible to deal with at such short notice. Dr. Blackmon understood, not pressuring them.

About ten days later, in the middle of the night, Mark woke Nancy up to tell her that he had made his decision; he was ready to proceed. He and Nancy would fly back to Rochester to get the first surgery taken care of; Dr. Blackmon would permanently close off the old fistulous or rotten bridge of tissue still attached to the stomach. That way it could never leak air—or anything else—back into the left chest cavity.

First, however, a 3-D CT scan model of Mark's anatomy had to be made since it was uniquely his; indeed, it was, as Nancy said in Caring-Bridge, "alien territory." His aortic anatomy was unique, with his ascending aorta rerouted to the right and patched with a graft.

In 2014, this 3-D CT was a Mayo state-of-the-art process which required over 100 hours to complete. It could not be done in Austin. Thus, Mark and Nancy made yet another trip to Rochester and returned to Austin to await surgery.

A week after the CT model was made, Mark and Nancy were once again headed back to Minnesota. The rest of our family closed out the summer for the kids, running to the pool and going to the snow cone stand; school was about to begin in a few weeks, and we shopped for shoes, paper, and pencils.

• • •

CHAPTER 38

AUGUST 12, 2014

THE THREE-HOUR PROCEDURE BEGAN AT St. Mary's Hospital at Mayo at 9:00 a.m. Marshall and Tabor stayed in Austin with Mark's family. I flew up to stay with Nancy while Mark was in the OR. I figured I'd arrive near the end of the surgery.

When I arrived, Mark was still in surgery after five hours. I could see the worry in Nancy's face. Dr. Blackmon stepped out shortly after I arrived. I had never met her before face to face, but she fit my mental image quite well. Slender in her scrubs, she spoke kindly and quietly but wasted no words. She told Nancy that they were not even close to being done. She drew us a schematic of what was going on. The black ink drawing was amazingly good; she must have seen it in my face because she mentioned with a laugh that she had been an art major at UT.

Dr. Blackmon showed Nancy and me how she had originally planned to ablate or destroy the inside of the rotten esophagus with a scope, removing as much of it as safely as possible. But this had turned out to be too risky: it was much too close to the rerouted and grafted aorta. That plan was scrapped.

Dr. Blackmon was now essentially removing the fistulous portion, piece by tiny piece, from the inside out and stapling the stomach off to detach the fistula from it. This was an excruciatingly slow process; scar tissue from Mark's chest surgeries in 2001 and 2013 presented the now-familiar challenge of having to destroy non-healthy adherent tissue while at the same time salvaging healthy tissue. She had even had to send a resident doctor out to get more special surgical supplies; damage in the chest cavity was far more extensive than even the 3-D CT had shown.

As we had heard in Mark's previous surgeries, scar tissue obliterated her view. Finally, she had to abandon using the endoscope and open a path through the upper abdomen. But there were adhesions and roadblocks there, too. Dr. Blackmon described it as a "concrete abdomen."

I thought at once of how Mark's surgeons in the past year had described his left chest surgical field. Dr. Kesler: "laborious" and "very labor-intensive." Dr. Estrera: "chiseling and "carving." And Dr. Khalil: "…completely frozen by scar tissue." Now the chest cavity was even more entangled with scar tissue, and Dr. Blackmon was forced to use an abdominal approach.

At first, I wondered how scar tissue had gotten into the abdominal cavity, but after some thought, it dawned on me how the same infectious process had probably leaked into the abdomen from the massively infected chest in September 2013.

In Mark's case, the proximal or near end of the esophagus had remained healthy and now emptied into the ostomy on his neck. It was the far end that had caused so much trouble. It seemed logical to me that the far-end infection had most likely compromised the area precisely where the esophagus passed through the diaphragm before entering the abdomen. Pus from that area most likely oozed south by gravity, infecting the top of the abdominal cavity as well. This upper abdomen then became very much like Mark's left chest cavity, forming impenetrable scar tissue.

These tissues Dr. Blackmon encountered were, once again, hard and brittle and broke easily, thus earning her apt description of "concrete abdomen." Even the gallbladder broke and a general surgeon had to be called in to remove it, causing even more delay. When Dr. Blackmon told us about this, we could tell she felt a bit chagrined. Nancy and I both assured her that in Mark's case, this was a given; we understood completely. She told us that abdominal pain was going to be expected after all the maneuvering she had been forced to do.

Nearly ten hours from start to finish, Mark came out of recovery without needing life support. He was in amazingly good spirits. Nancy asked Dr. Blackmon what to pray for; her answer, "healthy tissue."

The next day Mark was able to sit up in a chair. He had an abdominal drainage tube and his GJ-tube and ostomy bag remained. The drainage tube held clear fluid, for which we were all grateful. Three days after his surgery, Mark walked the hall five different times. He was allowed to use his G-tube port again for feeding. The next day, all IVs were removed. By August 17, Mark reported minimal pain and had no fever. All tests showed the operation to be a success; the fistula was gone forever. The tissue appeared to be healthy indeed. Mark and Nancy's goal was to get home before the kids started school. They barely made it, flying out on August 22.

CHAPTER 39

• • •

WITHIN A WEEK OF THEIR return, Mark was back at St. David's in downtown Austin to resume rehab. He was told he had had minimal backtracking on the progress on his right arm; his vision was actually better than before he had left for Mayo. Mark was happy but noted that what he really wanted was to be back at work.

Four weeks later, Mark's postoperative CT of both abdomen and chest were deemed "perfect" by Dr. Blackmon. The aortic graft remained intact and in good shape. The air pocket was gone. After much thought, Mark and Nancy decided that they were ready for a "normal" family year, free of hospitals, surgeries, and driving and flying thousands of miles for doctor visits and care. They targeted June 2015, as the return to Mayo for Dr. Blackmon's final esophageal reconstructive surgery. She agreed and assured them that surgery should be simple compared to all his previous ones.

For the first time in a year, Mark and Nancy visited Dell campus. There were hugs and handshakes all around. Mark's desk had been left untouched; family pictures were intact; he was still considered one of them. Dell had remained enormously supportive the entire time Mark had been gone, unable to work. They sent frequent emails and cards, and holiday gifts each Christmas. Coworkers would show up at the house to check up on his progress. Mark received his fifteen-year trophy through the mail when he was unable to be in the office to accept the award.

Back at rehab, Mark dealt with the part of his body that had thus far resisted most rehab attempts: his right arm and hand. A newfangled splint helped him extend his right wrist upward, since the paralysis had flexed it into a fist. Stubborn muscles were injected with Botox in seven areas to help loosen his arm and hand movements. These sessions would be repeated after several months. He worked with e-stim, electrical current to retrain the right arm nerve/muscle pathways to the brain. Hand weights were added. Sponge toys, pennies in a bowl, a soccer ball cut in half: despite every intervention, his right arm and hand stubbornly refused to change much. I watched Mark one time as he tried simply to turn off a single handle faucet with his right hand. He actually became short of breath and broke out in a sweat with both pain and effort. This was hard work, even after nearly a year had passed since his stroke.

October 2014 brought Marshall's ninth birthday. This year Mark could participate, instead of lying on the couch and watching through the window. A few weeks later, Mark's birthday celebration was a great improvement over the previous year's. Instead of being in the hospital, he had cake and ice cream on the back porch with family and friends. Thanksgiving weekend at the ranch, Mark got behind the wheel of his beloved red truck for the first time since his July 2013 surgery. He navigated the roads on the property with Wade's help; Nancy videoed his triumph.

Mark began to type with his left hand now that his vision and coordination were better; he spent at least five minutes daily on a special e-reader. Mark's good friend, Ron, another Dell computer wizard and long-time friend, visited and pitched in to help with inevitable electronic glitches.

By early December, Mark could type left-handed on the computer for up to an hour daily. The first word he typed completely on his own was *castle*. He shouted it downstairs to Nancy. His right arm was still nearly non-functional, however. He continued intense daily e-stim therapy; thirty minutes of daily homework was also devoted to his right hand and arm use. An even newer, complex state-of-the-art type of right-arm splint was designed for him. His labs were normal. Best of all, his cancer tumor marker numbers had remained totally normal since July 2013.

The month of December 2014 was designated a "therapy holiday." Mark worked at home, though, for up to two hours daily on the computer. As much as we all wanted the usual Christmas calendar as a gift, Mark was just not up to the complex compiling of a year's worth of photos. I noticed Elaine's latest Clifton calendar hanging in her back hall as if waiting for the time when Mark could produce a current one. It stayed unfolded to September 2013. Whenever I walked by it, I felt a sense of loss.

When Mark typed, left-handed, he achieved 60% accuracy on his own. There were more right hand Botox injections, yet his grasping abilities continued to be almost nil; he added a daily splint. Wonders and Worries came out to take a family photo; the Cliftons' story and photo would be on the cover of the organization's 2015 promotional pamphlet, due out in February.

Mark was getting stronger: he was able to sit through an entire basketball game at UT. This was no small feat; he had to have extra back support for sitting, since so many left ribs had been removed, but he could attend and enjoy. Wade and Elaine treated the family to Austin's Zilker Park to see the annual Christmas decorations; this too took stamina that Mark had not had until recently.

December 2014 was a huge milestone for the entire family. In seventeen months, Mark had gone from being totally incapacitated to beginning to function independently. This may seem almost intuitive, but it is anything but. Physically, now he could care for himself with ADLs, or activities of daily living, such as eating, using the bathroom, or getting dressed. He continued to improve mentally too, speaking more clearly, being better able to put thoughts together. But he still could not drive or return to work: two typically male markers of society. He wanted more than anything to be able to work; at that point, though, it was out of the question.

What about the other three family members? Nancy, of course, was wrung out, trying to be his caregiver and yet function as a wife and mom. She practically lived in her car, driving both the kids and Mark to place after place. Mark's parents and sisters helped out, but the addition of Mark's various therapies, haircuts, and massages ate into Nancy's time. She declared the dining room table as her office; there she dealt nearly daily with insurance companies, doctors' and hospitals' bills, denials and resubmissions of claims. All of this took a toll—sometimes a bill would not come until over a year after the procedure. Each error required long phone calls with explanations and delving into records, providing extra documentation or resubmission of claims. It was an unending and unpleasant task.

Tabor and Marshall had their issues, too. Davis Elementary had been most accommodating; Nancy had always volunteered there, and everyone knew what was going on at the Clifton's. On occasions, though, Tabor and Marshall would experience outbursts of frustration and anger, or homework not turned in. The kids continued at Wonders and Worries, too. Yet at times there were still problems with adjustment to the enormous blow this family unit had sustained.

It was like the Civil War; they had all survived the horror of war; now they were dealing with Reconstruction, trying to rebuild their family with a whole new set of parameters. Who's in charge? What role is each playing, and when? How can a marriage survive when two people are forced constantly to be together even when both so badly need a break? What are the consequences when early on, Mark had to rely on the kids for something as simple as finding the remote or cutting his meat?

Mark was aware of all this and felt sad that his health issues were at the root of much of it. He and Nancy discussed it at length and often: he had come so close to death so many times. He had endured excruciating pain, exhaustion, humiliation, frustration, fear, the sense of loss of his own freedom, yet he rarely complained and he never gave up. He wanted, as he often said, "to be happy and skillful." He just wasn't there yet, but he continued the struggle. Nancy, too, soldiered on, despite her own exhaustion. Both felt the daily weight of all they had to do and all they had yet to do. They rested when they could; then, they got up and did it all again.

CHAPTER 40

• • •

2015

IT WAS A NEW YEAR. February brought more therapy with the fancy right hand orthotic, forty-five minutes daily. Mark could read a bit; he continued typing left-handed. My son Tom flew in for a few days to help Mark with his computer. It was a geek fest with both men updating Mark's electronic toys: televisions, computers, modems, security cameras, remote controls, speakers. They had a great time. Nancy described Mark's overall health progress as "agonizingly slow." But it was progress.

By April, Mark's therapy was mainly at Austin Speech Labs, independently funded and not covered by insurance. He spent six hours a week there. His therapy was augmented at home with speech software from a company named Bungalow. Among other things, it worked with his word recall and gave directional clues for reading. He attended vision therapy too, working on eye movements and that right field neglect, among other issues. His cancer tumor markers remained normal.

The months dragged by as we prepared for the final journey to Mayo in July. In early June, Dr. Blackmon told Nancy and Mark that recovery time post-op would depend on how Mark healed. The plan was to pull the stomach up under the skin covering the breast bone and reconnect it with the stump that, at present, emptied into the ostomy bag on his neck. Another option included tunneling under the chest wall on the left. Nothing could be assured 100%; Mark was famous for scar tissue and the unique architecture on his aorta and left chest; he always presented unknown challenges when surgery was needed.

By the first week of July Mark had his preop blood work. It came as no surprise that he was somewhat dehydrated; after all, this was July in Texas. So, Nancy increased the amount of fluids she poured in through the G-tube port. Dr. Blackmon and her team went over and over the surgery to make ready.

My son Tom, Wade, and Elaine met Nancy and Mark at Mayo in Minnesota. We had rented a nearby lake house for a month so anyone could visit. Mark was going to have to stay in the hospital for two weeks and then for at least two more weeks after discharge.

He was once again admitted to St. Mary's Hospital, affiliated with Mayo. While Mark was in surgery, family members waiting in the hall noted a huge enlargement of a medical journal article, hanging on the wall. They recognized Dr. Blackmon's name as one of the authors. As they scanned the article, they realized they were reading about Mark, despite his name being blinded. There was even a picture of Mark's 3-D CT model in the article. This confirmed even more, how out of the ordinary Mark's case had always been. They sat down or paced to wait for yet another surgery to be over.

To no one's surprise, the straightforward surgery did not go as planned. First, adhesions again complicated the already intricate procedure. In her operative report, Dr. Blackmon noted that cutting them away took three hours. She and her team were unable to tunnel under the skin over the breast bone. Instead, they excavated to the left of the breast bone, forming a trough by removing pieces of his top two left ribs, part of the left collarbone, and part of the top left side of the breastbone. The option of using colon tissue to replace the far end of the esophagus was abandoned. Instead, the stomach itself was pulled up and protected by placing it into the channel created by the surgical team.

Repositioning the existing healthy top of the esophagus, where it had been rerouted to the neck ostomy two years before, proved to be challenging. The surgical team maneuvered and joined together the pulled-up stomach from below and the remaining healthy esophagus from the ostomy above. Once the team was convinced that they had a watertight continuous tube, they closed the ostomy site and made the final connection of all the various incision closures. This made a Y-shaped closure on Mark's left neck, which continued toward his breast bone and then down the entire length of his chest and abdomen. This huge, long closure was bolstered at ninety degrees every inch or so with pieces of thin but strong red tubing. It looked like a grotesque train track.

The complex and delicate manipulation of the ostomy site created quite a tight fit in Mark's upper left chest and neck. Plastic surgery members of the team were at first concerned about some swelling around the area where the ostomy site was revised, but after the surgery, they all were comfortable that it was a success. The two-hour surgery took six hours.

On July 11, the day after surgery, Dr. Blackmon and the plastics team described the final incision closure as "beautiful"; the swelling was gone. The site was clean and healthy-looking. OT was begun on Mark's right arm; he even took a walk with physical therapy. Dr. Blackmon told Nancy that our job as a family was to distract Mark from the pain he was certain to experience.

Think of the excruciating pain associated with breaking a rib; Mark had already lost parts of six left back ribs; now he had lost parts of two more left front ribs as well as parts of his left collarbone and left upper breastbone. Simply breathing, moving the rib cage, was painful; sitting up was even worse at first since the chest cage's left front uppermost support was now compromised. But at least he was going to be able to eat again soon; the ostomy was gone, and the feeding tube would be gone after he was stable and gaining weight again.

Mark had to have a PICC line placed again since his veins were so fragile; he was still a bit dehydrated and fluids were pushed. He also developed an elevated white blood cell count, and antibiotics were started. His tube feeds were begun again, but they caused pain and had to be stopped. Hiccups were more of a problem than was expected and sapped his energy. He continued to walk and to have the hiccups, but not to the extent as in 2013. After he was given a bath and cleaned up, he declared he felt a thousand percent better. He walked some more.

In one week, the plastics team signed off his case since his skin was healing well. Several days later, his heart monitor and IV lines were discontinued in preparation for discharge. On post-op day nine, Mark was wheeled outdoors into the courtyard, which he enjoyed.

The dietary team helped Nancy to plan for feeding at the lake house where they would stay for two weeks; Mark was still on his formula by G-port, but after another week and some tests, he was expected to take his first oral nourishment in two years. He was anxious for that day to come.

He even handled stairs at the hospital as he was preparing for discharge. At the lake house, family members came and went. I flew in with Tabor and Marshall; Wade, Elaine, and Tom went home. On July 21, Mark was discharged from St. Mary's.

The next week was spent trying to replace the weight that Mark had lost in the hospital. The problem was that he was unable to handle the usual eight daily cans of tube feeding. We were unsure why, but we guessed it was due to the stomach's trauma of being pulled up and stretched all the way up to the top of his left chest cavity. He still, of course, relied on nourishment via G-tube. Pain was much greater than he had expected, too.

The more discomfort Mark felt, the more he had to have pain meds, which stopped up his entire gastrointestinal tract, causing additional pain. Sitting upright was itself uncomfortable. The huge incision caused pressure and discomfort. He began to wonder if all this was worth it, after all.

When Mark and Nancy went back to Mayo to see Dr. Blackmon on July 27, she told him that the increased pain was not a surprise. She explained how much had been done in rearranging his anatomy, all of which added to the pain. She had found wires in his abdomen from previous chest surgeries and had to remove them. She had even encountered a pinched and twisted area of the small intestine and had to disentangle it. In addition to having his stomach pulled up, all the lysis or cutting away of adhesions, tunneling, cutting ribs, collarbone, and breastbone, and reattaching the viable piece of his esophagus were pain-inducing. It had not been simple, for sure. She assured him that once the sutures and bolster tubing were removed, he should feel much better, and she was right.

Even in the exam room, Mark heaved a sigh of relief once Dr. Blackmon freed him from sutures and bolsters. But it was not yet over; he had yet to pass a swallowing test to ensure that the esophagus was intact; only then could he begin to eat normally.

Two days later, Mark passed his swallowing test, as well as a nerve test performed on his left hand. He had had some tingling in his left hand, probably from leaning on his left elbow in bed, since his right arm still couldn't support his weight. The test was normal.

When the testing was over, Mark had to swallow some water at the hospital. Nancy held her breath, excited when Mark swallowed and then shot her a tiny smile and said, "What's the big deal? It's only water." No choking or sputtering: it was a big deal, indeed.

At the lake house, he requested broccoli cheese soup for his first meal. Nancy videoed him as he said, "Oh, that's good, that's good!" Later that year, her video was expanded with clinical detail from Mayo and shown on the Austin evening news during Christmas time.

Finally, on August 1, 2015, Mark and Nancy flew home to Austin. Family and friends joined in the rejoicing. Mark had requested egg salad for his first meal under his own roof. I headed to the kitchen and lovingly prepared this simple dish, even checking the computer to be sure it would be perfect for such a momentous event.

It wasn't.

CHAPTER 41

• • •

I HAD USED LOW-FAT MAYONNAISE in the egg salad, which caused excruciating abdominal pain. We were all so afraid he'd throw up—what would that do to a two-week-old suture line? As he walked about and belched (a new phenomenon), he gradually felt better.

Now the hunt was on: what could he eat that he would like, that would not cause abdominal discomfort, and yet would fulfill the daily 2,600-calorie, high protein requirement? Oh, and no high-sugar foods either, which could promote vomiting. Further, Nancy had to calculate and measure every calorie, since she was to decrease his tube feeding by the same number of calories he took in orally every day. The detailed nutrition discharge instructions ran for pages with ideas and calculation short-cuts. In no time at all, those pages were ragged with re-reading and dotted with food spills.

It sounds simple, and in theory, it is; the devil was in putting it into action six times a day. The problem was getting Mark to eat or drink high calorie, high protein, low sugar drinks. He hated them all. We combed health food stores, the aisles of every big-box food store and grocery store, and online websites. Mark was unhappy with nearly every food and literally could not stomach it. He wanted real food, like meat. Like queso! Yet he was to have no bread, sushi, big pieces of barbeque, or steak for a year. Fatty foods had to be replaced with high protein ones. Nancy made smoothies and milkshakes, but to no avail. He liked some of them but could tolerate very little at a time.

Nancy used her blender to make tiny pieces of meat; even though it tasted good, it was still hard to digest. We tried baby food: *nope*. A visit to the nutritionist was not helpful; she was used to helping people lose weight. A second nutritionist was not what was needed, either; he suggested huge-sized supplements, but Mark was not allowed to swallow large pills at all. His esophageal opening was at present about a centimeter, less than half an inch, in diameter.

Which led to another problem. One of his generic heart medicines, when crushed, was abhorrent to Mark's taste buds. This made perfect sense: all previous crushed pills had been put into his GJ-tube; he had not tasted any of it. Nancy tried hiding it in small tastes of everything: peanut butter, jelly, ice cream, pudding. *Nope.*

Mark's heart medicine had to be changed to a similar dosage of a smaller tablet, just to get it down. Nancy found that he could take all his pills, one at a time, if he dipped them in pudding; she added coconut oil to his pudding to dilute out the sugar and increase the calories.

Slowly, Mark's diet progressed to the things he loved: queso, refried beans, broccoli cheese soup, peanut butter, tiny bits of blender-shredded beef. But the quantities he could tolerate were so small that he was unable to reach his 2,600-calorie daily goal. Despite all this effort, he still did not gain any weight. Both Nancy and Mark were frustrated. Mealtime was increasingly a challenge.

Sometimes the only solution to getting 2,600 calories into Mark every twenty-four hours was for Nancy to speed up his last tube feeding and run it for up to ten hours at night. Even that would cause bloating or diarrhea if it went too fast.

Five days after returning home, Mark returned to rehab; he had more Botox injections into his right arm and hand. This increase in activity used up the precious calories Nancy pumped into him; his weight stayed at 162. He finally did reach his caloric goal, but it required his eating rich ice cream daily. He loved that, and he was blessed by being able to tolerate it at long last. Ten unending and frustrating weeks after surgery, Mark was finally able to retain his 163 pounds via oral feedings exclusively for seven days in a row. It was time to ditch the GJ-tube.

CHAPTER 42

• • •

ON SEPTEMBER 2, 2015, I had the honor of removing Mark's feeding tube. The sutures holding it in place had become embedded in the skin, so I first applied pain-killing ointment. That wasn't much help, but he was stoic. Soon he was ecstatic at no longer having the tube poking out of his abdomen. Marshall and Tabor made a video of throwing away his syringes, medicine mixing equipment, IV pole, the now-rusty muffin tin, and the last of his cans of tube feedings. It was a red-letter day at the Clifton household!

To celebrate, I took Mark and Marshall to a midnight Star Wars promotion; Nancy and Tabor, although fans, wisely declined. This was a big deal for both guys. Mark warned Marshall that no matter how tired he was, he had to go to school the next day without complaint. Marshall gave Mark a high-five.

For Mark, it was a challenge since he knew standing in line would be required. Long lines of people snaked near the front windows of the store, mostly adults. By the time we left, we had spent an entire hour at the event. Mark handled standing up the whole time without complaint. He had a big smile on his face as he stepped into the car: he had gotten some treasures he had wanted, and he had gone the distance. Marshall went to school the next day tired but content.

The days turned into weeks. Mark was now back at therapy five days a week; this included speech, occupational, and vision therapy. Getting to and from appointments again took master planning for Nancy and family members. Mark tried Uber and after learning the system, could call them on his cell, freeing up Nancy even more. Then, Uber was no longer available in Austin and it was back to square one.

Now that the feeding tube was removed, Mark could swim at St. David's pool, exercising his right arm muscles even more, but just at that point, the system closed the facility, so that was put on hold. Bob, his therapist, suggested that he consider trying the hospital's driving training, using adaptive equipment on the wheel and retraining his left foot to operate the pedals. That was exciting news.

Six weeks ran by, one much like the other. At the ranch at Thanksgiving, Mark again drove his red truck but was disappointed to find his right foot had trouble with the brake pedal. Driving was put on hold once again. On December 25, Mark ate his first Christmas meal in two years; what a pleasure! My son Tom visited again, and the two repeated their geek fest of electronic toys.

Eventually, Mark's CaringBridge site received 25,841 hits. Nancy stopped posting on December 29, 2015. Mark's success story continued, but his gains were less obvious. He could do household chores like dishes and laundry, he could navigate on his computer with games and videos, yet to be equal to the Mark of 2013 was still a long way away.

In the spring of 2016, the Cliftons took their first family vacation in four years. When I picked them up from the airport, I could sense at once that some family healing had taken place in just the few days they were away. Mark took much more initiative in being head of household, getting luggage out of the car, helping with other chores that usually fell to Nancy alone. All of them had big smiles and much to talk about; it was a pleasure to observe them.

Multiple times over the year, the question of the future arose. A sense of "now what?" pervaded the family's daily lives. They attended counseling as a family to gain a sense of perspective. Tabor was now a tween, attending middle school further from home. Next year, Marshall would no longer be at Davis Elementary. As Nancy's role in volunteering at the kids' schools lessened, she pulled out her resume, planning to go back to work. What implications would all these things have for the family, Mark in particular?

Throughout 2016, Mark continued in his speech therapy several times weekly. Although his speech became more fluent, its cadence was slow. There remains even now a remnant of the aphasia, making him struggle for the word he wants; at times apraxia still trips him up, making words like "supposedly" difficult to enunciate. He is on his feet independently, but going to work and driving are still beyond his reach, both of which annoy him immensely.

In the meantime, Mark has learned to prepare his own breakfast and lunch when Nancy is busy with the kids; all four still eat dinner together. He keeps up with his vision therapy homework, which ends in 2017. In October 2016, he was freed from the training eyepatch: a significant milestone. Like any other parent, he attends Tabor's band concerts and Marshall's Wednesday school lunches. With help from his Dell friend, Ron, Mark continues to relearn and to update the intricate home computer system and other electronics he had interconnected before 2013. Tweaking them is a daily activity.

In November 2016, Mark told Nancy he wanted to re-open the hot tub; when they took the cover off they found only fetid water and grime. Nancy's dad spent several days cleaning and repairing it; afterward Nancy snapped a picture of Mark, Tabor, and Marshall lounging in the now-pristine hot tub. Another milestone.

In early 2017, Nancy found a part-time job where she could work mostly from home. Near that same time, Mark told Nancy he was ready to start on the Christmas 2017 calendar. Another milestone! Nancy found him a lightweight duffel bag he uses to swing over his shoulder to carry laundry upstairs. In late February, she noticed he was moving his right arm more than before. He even posted a CaringBridge entry, typical of his humor: "I'm still not dead." It had been over a year since Nancy had posted. More milestones! Most importantly, Mark's tumor markers have consistently come back normal; he remains cancer free.

Much life work remains for the Cliftons, of course. Memories of so many ghastly times can be haunting; planning when there is no way to predict the future is beyond frustrating. Every day presents some new challenge; all four of them continue to wrestle with those challenges and to move forward, not back.

How does Mark keep going? Dr. Baptiste, who saved his life in 2013 both on September 16th and 19th, put it perfectly: "He's like Audie Murphy: he's been to hell and back." It was also Dr. Baptiste who described Mark with the terms "grit and grace."

The Mark I know is not afraid to try anything to regain his independence. His goal is to go back to work; he's not afraid to fail along the way, but he definitely refuses to accept defeat. He just smiles and says he's got a lot yet to do. He acknowledges all the prayers and kindnesses of countless people, many of whom he's never met. He loves his family and wants to be a part of it, just as he's always done. And, yes, he plans to grow old with Nancy.

Mark with Baxter and Beau 5/12/13

Maine vacation: Tabor, Henry Gustavson, Carol
Werner Gustavson, Nancy, Mark, Judy,
Rosie Cario Werner, Tom Werner, Marshall 6/18/13

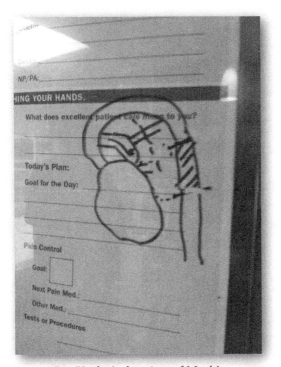

Dr. Kesler's drawing of Mark's
left chest surgery 7/19/13

Mark on life support with Tabor, Nancy, and Marshall 9/25/13

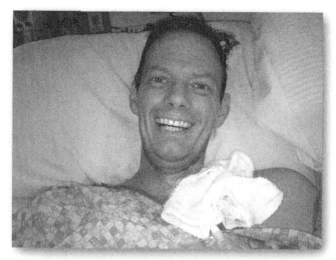

Mark off life support 10/4/13

Mark in wheelchair, hospitalized again 11/25/13

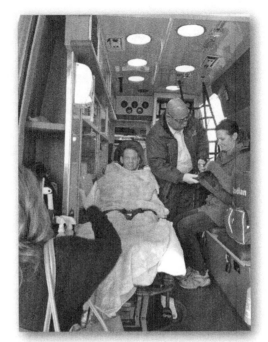

Nancy with Mark, transferred by ambulance
from Austin to Houston, 12/10/13

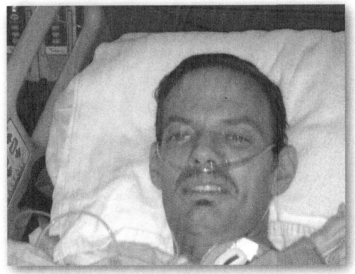

Mark in Hermann Hospital, Houston, after his stroke 12/28/13

Marshall with Mark at TIRR 2/22/14

Tabor, Mark, Marshall home again in Austin 3/18/14

Mark with Beau, convalescent
canine companion 4/6/14

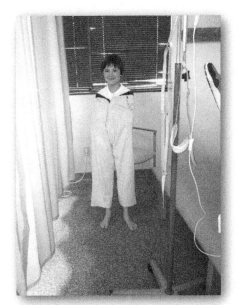

Marshall keeping warm in Mark's warm-up
slacks, physical therapy 5/5/14

Mark walking after chest surgery,
Mayo in Minnesota 8/15/14

Mark introduces Tabor to the trombone he
played in high school and college 1/18/15

Mark and Tabor do vision therapy:
find the chocolate 4/19/15

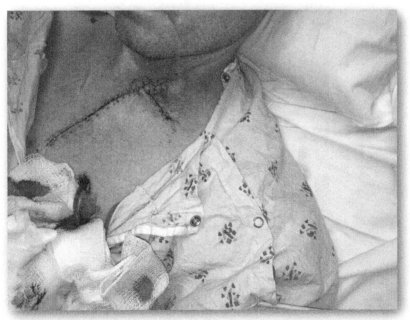

Mark's ostomy site reversal and esophagus reconstruction, postop 7/12/15

Mark, healed and home, with Nancy 10/13/15

Marshall and Tabor in front, Judy, Nancy, and
Mark behind at Star Wars movie 12/21/15

Now retired, Dr. Judith K. Werner was a high school and college English instructor before changing careers to become a board-certified family physician.

After a decade spent teaching, Werner enrolled at the University of North Texas Medical School, graduating with a doctor of osteopathy degree in 1986. She then worked as an intern at Fort Worth Osteopathic Hospital and completed a family-practice residency at Methodist Hospital Systems of Dallas, Texas.

Werner practiced medicine for twenty-four years and was elected the first female president of medical staff at Methodist Health Systems of Dallas in 2000.

A mother of three and grandmother of five, Werner lives in Cedar Hill, Texas. She is training her Great Pyrenees, Teddy, to be a therapy animal and looks forward to walking hospital corridors with a white dog instead of in a white coat.

Thank you for buying this book.
All proceeds will go to Tabor's and
Marshall's college funds.

Made in the USA
Monee, IL
07 February 2023

26848670R00105